# At Issue

# Food Safety

# Other Books in the At Issue Series:

# At Issue

# Food Safety

*Judeen Bartos, Book Editor*

**GREENHAVEN PRESS**
*A part of Gale, Cengage Learning*

GALE
CENGAGE Learning

Detroit • New York • San Francisco • New Haven, Conn • Waterville, Maine • London

GALE
CENGAGE Learning

Christine Nasso, *Publisher*
Elizabeth Des Chenes, *Managing Editor*

© 2011 Greenhaven Press, a part of Gale, Cengage Learning.

Gale and Greenhaven Press are registered trademarks used herein under license.

*For more information, contact:*
Greenhaven Press
27500 Drake Rd.
Farmington Hills, MI 48331-3535
Or you can visit our Internet site at gale.cengage.com

For product information and technology assistance, contact us at

Gale Customer Support, 1-800-877-4253
For permission to use material from this text or product, submit all requests online at www.cengage.com/permissions

Further permissions questions can be emailed to permissionrequest@cengage.com

Articles in Greenhaven Press anthologies are often edited for length to meet page requirements. In addition, original titles of these works are changed to clearly present the main thesis and to explicitly indicate the author's opinion. Every effort is made to ensure that Greenhaven Press accurately reflects the original intent of the authors. Every effort has been made to trace the owners of copyrighted material.

Cover Image copyright © Images.com/Corbis.

**LIBRARY OF CONGRESS CATALOGING-IN-PUBLICATION DATA**

Food safety / Judeen Bartos, book editor.
p. cm. -- (At issue)
Includes bibliographical references and index.
ISBN 978-0-7377-5149-9 (hardcover) -- ISBN 978-0-7377-5150-5 (pbk.)
1. Food--Juvenile literature. 2. Food--Safety measures--Juvenile literature. I. Bartos, Judeen. II. Title. III. Series.
TX355.F57 2011
363.19'2--dc22

2010043628

# Contents

# Introduction

Americans worried about the safety and nutritional value of their foods are exploring alternatives to the status quo, and questioning the food safety system charged with regulating the nation's food supply. A growing sense of urgency led Congress pass legislation in late 2010 placing tighter restrictions on food producers and processors and the overhaul of a system that has not seen substantive reform in over a century. President Barack Obama has called keeping our food supply safe "a fundamental responsibility of government," and pledges to back funding increases to institute these reforms.

But not all groups welcome these changes. Critics question whether increased government regulation interferes with an individual's freedom of choice, however healthy or not those choices may be. "In America I have the freedom to own guns, speak and assemble," says Joel Salatin in his essay published in the book *Food, Inc.* "But what good are those freedoms if I can't choose to eat what my body wants in order to have the energy to shoot, preach, and worship?"

The controversial aspect of changes to the food safety system is exemplified in the ongoing battle surrounding cow's milk, a long time staple of many Americans' diets. Until the early 1900s, all milk was 'raw' milk—the present-day term for milk that comes straight from a cow or goat and is consumed without any processing. There were no methods for treating milk for possible contaminants or disease and milk was responsible for one quarter of all food-borne illnesses. But using a method pioneered by Louis Pasteur in the 1800s, later known as pasteurization, scientists experimented with heating milk to try and kill the germs that were causing people to get sick. Pasteurizing milk proved successful in stopping the spread of several diseases, including tuberculosis and typhoid fever, and by the 1950s pasteurization was a federal standard for all commercially sold milk. But pasteurizing milk does have a downside. Along with killing germs in the milk, the process also kills some of milk's nutrients.

Other processes have been developed since then to enhance the quality and safety of milk, including homogenization, microfiltration, and ultrapasteurization. As milk becomes increasingly engineered beyond its natural form, a growing faction of critics contend that these enhancements are decreasing the nutritional benefits of milk and contributing to increases in the number of children with allergies and milk intolerances. Others point out the seeming connections between the rise of antibiotic resistant strains of bacteria and the increased use of antibiotics in cows.

In 1993, a recombinant bovine growth hormone (rBGH) developed by the Monsanto Corporation was offered to dairy farmers as a way to increase the milk output of their cows. Some studies have shown a link between rBGH and cancer in humans and the outcry against the genetically engineered hormone was widespread. Several countries, including Australia, Canada and Japan, banned the sale of milk containing rBGH shortly after its introduction. Consumer reaction in the United States has pressured many large retailers such as Wal-Mart and Starbucks to commit to not purchasing milk containing rBGH. While the backlash against the growth hormone has been fierce, the U.S. Food and Drug Administration (FDA) remains steadfast in its assertions that rBGH milk is not harmful to consumers.

A growing number of Americans feel that too often consumers have become the guinea pigs for products that have not been properly tested. They are concerned about how far from their natural origins many foods have strayed, and are using their food dollars to promote more organic selections, which are free of additives and pesticides, and, in the case of milk, are choosing raw milk for their families.

The trend of choosing to drink raw milk has created great controversy. The FDA maintains that raw milk is a health threat and the sale of it has been banned in several states, effectively turning the people who want to sell and purchase raw milk into criminals. Raw milk advocates point out that there is a greater penalty for its sale and purchase than there is for cigarettes and alcohol, both of which, they say, have been proven to present far more risk to a person's health than raw milk. They cite numerous examples, based on anecdotal evidence, of children and adults experiencing fewer illnesses and allergies after switching to raw milk.

However, few scientific studies have been able to back these claims and raw milk has sickened over one thousand people since 1998. Raw milk was responsible for an outbreak of *E.coli* and campylobacter in July 2010 in Colorado that sickened twenty-four people and sent two children to the hospital. Still, those who believe the health benefits of raw milk outweigh these risks argue that they have the right to choose what foods they eat, and feel that the laws are an infringement on their individual rights. They feel a middle ground can be reached by putting a warning label on raw milk products and requiring strict safety standards in the handling and testing of the milk. David Acheson, a former FDA associate commissioner working for the agency until 2009, concurs with the compromise approach. He currently works as the Managing Director of Food and Import Safety at Leavitt Partners. He writes in the company's blog on May 12, 2010: "The battle over raw milk will continue to result in a public health stalemate until the intellectual capital of those involved in the argument moves to a different level and looks for collaborative solutions not confrontational ones."

As the controversy surrounding milk shows, Americans remain divided over how many restrictions they are willing to tolerate in the name of food safety, and government continues to wrestle with revamping existing regulations in a way that keeps our food supply safe, encourages healthy eating habits, and also respects the rights of individuals.

1

# Lack of Food Safety Is an Imminent Threat to American Families

*Andrew Kimbrell*

*Andrew Kimbrell is the Executive Director of the Center for Food Safety. He is a public interest attorney and activist, and the author of several books, including* Your Right to Know: Genetic Engineering and the Secret Changes in Your Food, *published in 2007. Kimbrell has lectured at numerous universities and has appeared on* The Today Show, Good Morning America, *and* Crossfire.

*A broken food safety system has resulted in an alarming rate of food-borne related illnesses and deaths, with little being done to prevent future outbreaks. Lack of regulation has allowed the quality and long-term safety of our food supply to deteriorate as dangerous chemicals permeate even what are considered healthy food options, such as fruit and vegetables. Food choices advertised to our children and provided as part of federal school lunch programs have contributed to poor health for our youngest citizens. Further, even as the controversy over the potential health hazards of genetically modified foods continues, history repeats as untested nano-technological based foods are rushed to market. Congress appears poised to act to address the growing lack of confidence in America's food safety system, but struggles against the pressures of agribusiness lobbyists who wish to maintain the profitable status quo, and against the regulatory overlaps be-*

*tween various agencies. Nothing less than systemic change that consolidates authority under one agency committed solely to issues of food safety will reverse the course of America's defective food safety framework.*

The United States once had one of the safest food systems in the world, but now, 70 million Americans are sickened, 300,000 are hospitalized, and 5,000 die from food-borne illness every year. It is a sad fact: since 9/11 [2001], far more Americans have been killed, injured or hurt because of our lack of a coordinated food safety system than by terrorist acts that challenge our Homeland Security system.

The culprits in this assault on American wellbeing aren't shadowy terrorist figures, but rather, they are what most consumers would identify as wholesome—not harmful—foods. Peanuts, lettuce, pistachios, spinach, hamburgers sold to Boy Scout camps, peppers, tomatoes, and pepper-coated sausages are among the foods that have sickened and killed Americans in just the last few years. Our children are most at risk from these food threats, with half of all food-borne illness striking children under 15 years old.

---

*Illnesses caused by contaminated foods, which could be prevented with proper government oversight, are instead causing the hospitalization of hundreds of thousands and the deaths of thousands of Americans.*

---

## Funding Cuts Result in Fewer Inspections

The [George W.] Bush administration constantly claimed it was protecting Americans from potential security threats, yet it completely failed to protect the public from the clear and present danger of deadly food.

Due in part to that administration's cuts in funding and staff, the Food and Drug Administration (FDA) currently inspects less than 25% of all food facilities in the U.S. More than 50% of all American food facilities have gone uninspected for five years or more. During President Bush's last term, regulatory actions against those companies selling contaminated food to Americans declined by over a half.

The result is tragically predictable. Large processing facilities, which now mix foods from across the country and the world, are not being inspected. Illnesses caused by contaminated foods, which could be prevented with proper government oversight, are instead causing the hospitalization of hundreds of thousands and the deaths of thousands of Americans. Again, the victims are, disproportionately, our children.

The tens of millions of victims of food-borne illness represent only one segment of the casualties from our failure to require safe and nutritious food. Because of lax regulation of agricultural chemicals, many of the fruits and vegetables that should bring us health and nutrition are instead laced with dangerous pesticides, dozens of which are known carcinogens. Much of the food marketed to our children and served in their schools are confections brimming with trans-fats and high-fructose corn syrup; these contribute mightily to the epidemic of obesity in the young and heart disease and diabetes in our older populations. Under pressure from agribusiness, our federal agencies and legislators continue to commercialize genetically modified foods with no safety testing and no labeling for consumers. And, despite the strong potential of health hazards, foods made with new, nanotechnology-based chemicals are getting waived through to the market, without any independent testing at all.

## Congress Acts to Address Growing Concerns

Clearly our food safety system is broken and needs a complete overhaul. With the continuing string of food contamination scandals, even Congress has begun to pay attention. The Food

Safety Enhancement Act (HR 2749) was passed by the House of Representatives in the summer of 2008 and takes some steps in the right direction. It gives more authority to the FDA, restoring some of its power to conduct food inspections and strengthen oversight.

However, it's far from perfect. Bowing to pressure from agribusiness, lawmakers have exempted livestock producers and any other entity regulated by the USDA [United States Department of Agriculture] from the new regulations of both this act and its Senate companion, the Food Safety Modernization Act (S.510). In fact, members of Congress were so committed to the interests of big industrial meat producers that they also prohibited the FDA from "impeding, minimizing, or affecting" USDA authority on meat, poultry, and eggs. As a result, these bills contain the stupefying provision that no attempt by the FDA to combat E. coli and Salmonella will be allowed. These bacteria are the most common causes of deadly food-borne illness and are found in products contaminated with animal feces. Since January 2010, over 850,000 pounds of beef—mostly from industrial feed lots—has been recalled due to E. coli O157:H7 contamination. The members of Congress have essentially protected the interests of corporations who are bad actors, while condemning the public to continued sickness from these contaminants.

Another major problem with both bills is that they begin with the flawed premise that all producers and processors of food—whether massive corporate farms or small family farms—are equally at fault for our broken food safety system. New food safety legislation should target the largest causes of food-borne illness. These include concentrated animal feeding operations (CAFOs), water and field contamination due to manure lagoon leakage, and industrial processing systems, not small farms.

The "one size fits all" regulatory approach in these bills fails to take this disparity into account. It instead places an undue and unsupportable burden on family farms, small processors, and direct marketers of organic and locally grown food. These have not been contributors to the contamination events which have caused major food-borne illness outbreaks. Further support for this view is that, at a July 2009 House Oversight Subcommittee on Domestic Policy hearing on Ready-to-Eat Vegetables and Leafy Green Agreements, then-Senior FDA Adviser Michael R. Taylor acknowledged that "since 1999 outbreaks of food-borne pathogens were traced to leafy greens involved in precut packaged leafy greens and not whole leafy greens".

## Proposed Legislation Does Not Address Fundamental Issues

It is unconscionable that factory farms would get a pass under the proposed legislation while family farmers, who often struggle to stay in operation, are held to stringent, unnecessary and potentially bankrupting requirements. Small operators would bear the brunt of large fees that generate the revenue sufficient for the overall food safety program to operate. Food safety regulation at the farm and processing level must be appropriate to scale and level of risk.

*It is long overdue that we establish a separate and effective government agency dedicated to food safety.*

Fortunately, some Senators are addressing the gaps in their bill. Perhaps the most critical action so far is that of Sen. John Tester (D-MT), who has introduced an amendment to exempt small-scale and direct marketing farmers and processors, who are already well regulated by local authorities.

However, most problematic is that the legislation in its current state perpetuates the regulatory tangle that is our food safety system. Arcane mixes of regulatory authority between the FDA, USDA and EPA [Environmental Protection Agency] make for dangerously inefficient government. It is long over-due that we establish a separate and effective government agency dedicated to food safety. We need to separate out the 'Food' part of the Food and Drug Administration and consolidate all authority under a new Food Safety Agency.

We did this for Homeland Security; we should also do it for food security. After all, it is the lack of food safety in this country that is the far more imminent threat to all of us, our families and, especially, our children.

# 2

# Additional Food Regulation Is Not Needed

*David E. Gumpert*

*David E. Gumpert is a journalist who focuses on health and business topics. He has written a number of books, including* The Raw Milk Revolution: Behind America's Emerging Battle over Food Rights.

*Well-publicized cases of food-borne illnesses involving contaminated spinach, peanut butter, pistachios and other products have served to highlight the deficiencies of the Food and Drug Administration in handling large-scale outbreaks. Although tragic, it is unknown whether these incidents represent an upward trend because data on food-borne illnesses is lacking. Pending legislation seeks to increase the powers of the FDA to handle food safety, but those powers will infringe upon the rights of individuals and impose undue financial burdens on small food producers.*

There have been all kinds of scary headlines and stories about food safety problems. The most recent was a front-page story in the *New York Times* a few weeks ago about a young dance instructor who wound up paralyzed from the waist down after a bout of illness from E.coli O157:H7 contained in a hamburger she ate. The story led to so much public upset that Agriculture Secretary Tom Vilsack was prompted to issue a statement saying the case was "unacceptable and tragic."

Shortly after that, victims of foodborne illness were received by [Barack] Obama administration officials at the White House for a high-profile photo session.

Besides health care reform, new food safety legislation moving through Congress (passed by the House, about to be voted on by the Senate) is billed as the most urgent consumer proposal in the Congress. It's supposed to reduce the scary headlines about contaminated peanut butter, pistachios, ground beef, spinach, and other foods that have embarrassed the public health establishment over the last three years.

Unlike health care reform, food safety legislation, which is designed to give the U.S. Food and Drug Administration [FDA] more power to monitor food producers and institute recalls, is heavily supported by an array of consumer organizations and health industry professionals, not to mention bureaucrats and legislators. President Obama has indicated he's ready to sign whatever Congress passes.

## Is Foodborne Illness a Growing Problem?

But in all the handwringing, there's been very little data presented by public health officials to document that we have a worsening problem with foodborne illness. Indeed, when you review the testimony provided by the FDA and other experts to the House in connection with the legislation that passed there over the summer [of 2009], no one even tried to make a statistical case that we have a worsening problem with foodborne illness. The best you'll find is FDA food safety adviser Michael R. Taylor, saying, "Every year, millions of our friends and neighbors in the United States suffer from foodborne illness, hundreds of thousands are hospitalized, and thousands die."

The reason FDA experts haven't provided more convincing data is that it doesn't exist. Indeed, if you examine the data on foodborne illness, you find a different sort of crisis—a crisis of credibility, based on ineffective and incomplete data gathering and investigation. And some of what is there actually shows declines in rates of foodborne illness.

## Available Data Is Suspect

The bastion of data on foodborne illness is the U.S. Centers for Disease Control and Prevention [CDC], and the data it pushes the public to consider as most relevant is a study scientists conducted more than ten years ago, and published in 1999. The study estimates that 76 million Americans are sickened by foodborne illness each year, with 325,000 hospitalizations and 5,000 deaths. (That's the data the FDA's Michael Taylor was quoting from.)

Three things are most notable about this data. First, it is old. Not only is the paper containing its findings more than ten years old, but the data it draws on goes back to as far as 1948.

Second, it is based entirely on what can only be termed wild estimates of the real situation. The number of reported illnesses are miniscule in comparison with the 76 million estimate. Even allowing for the multiplier effect—the likelihood that for every reported illness, there may be between ten and forty times that number not reported—the numbers don't obviously add up to the millions projected by the CDC. Consider that in 2007, the CDC reported a total 21,183 cases of foodborne illness, based on reports from states and localities around the country. Multiplying that by 40, you still only get 847,000 illnesses, a far cry from 76 million.

Not only that, but the 2007 data of reported illnesses is down 15% from the 25,035 reported in 2001. The Center for Science and the Public Interest, a nonprofit organization that also monitors foodborne illnesses, reported last year that it counted 168,000 illnesses over the 17-year period 1990–2006. That averages out to fewer than 10,000 per year.

The problem here isn't that the CDC is manipulating the data, but rather that the data is incomplete. Public health offi-

cials will tell you that states categorize illnesses differently, and vary widely in their aggressiveness in seeking out information. The Center for Science and the Public Interest in its 2008 report on foodborne illness reported that "nearly half of all states do not follow national standards for tracking disease outbreaks. Those gaps are particularly troubling given the numerous recent large outbreaks."

## New FDA Powers Increase Costs, Paperwork for Small Businesses

So what's behind the hysteria on foodborne illness? Clearly, part of it has to do with the dramatic cases being reported of individuals who have suffered serious long-term repercussions. While the vast majority of foodborne illnesses involve mild gastrointestinal problems that last just a few days, the serious cases obviously capture public attention, and stir up nervousness, as well they should. They are tragic.

> *It would seem that the FDA should at least put together data showing the nature of the foodborne illness problem at hand, and to what extent its new powers will solve the problem.*

But there's another factor at work here as well: a drive to broadly expand the powers of the FDA. As one example, it will have the power under the House legislation recently passed to require highly detailed written food plans from all food producers, including the smallest makers of artisan cheese and meats. The owner of a two-person California maker of specialty cheeses, fruits, and nuts, told me that creating such a plan would require about 100 hours of upfront work, and then two hours a day to be kept up to date. Failure to comply could result in a fine of $10,000 per infraction per day, this for a business doing less than $100,000 of annual revenues.

In addition, the FDA could inspect the records of all food producers at will, instead of the current requirement of having strong reason to believe a problem exists, or obtaining a search warrant. It will also be able to quarantine large areas of the country if it believes a serious source of pathogens exist, and shut down all food shipping in the process. And it will obtain substantial additional budget for inspection personnel.

Before requiring such an infringement on individual rights, and added costs for doing business, it would seem that the FDA should at the least put together data showing the nature of the foodborne-illness problem at hand, and to what extent its new powers will solve the problem. It could be that more targeted changes, costing less in funding for new personnel and foregone rights, could be quite effective in reducing foodborne illnesses.

3

# Regulation Is Necessary
# for Food Safety

*Nancy Scola*

*Nancy Scola has written for the* American Prospect, Politics
Magazine, Columbia Journalism Review, *and* Alternet, *in ad-
dition to* Science Progress. *She has also worked for the Personal
Democracy Forum and provided commentary for the BBC, Air
America, and CNN.*

*Recent proposed legislation would make several simple but far-
reaching changes to the way America's food system is run. One
of these is in the area of food traceability. Improved traceability
that indicates the specific origin of contaminated food can reduce
the number of blanket recalls that take place, during which every
food producer, guilty or innocent, is adversely affected. The use
of a tiered approach to facility inspections is another valuable
tool—high-risk sites would receive far more visits and focus than
low-risk locations. Additionally, the U.S. Food and Drug Administration (FDA) should take an increasingly thoughtful and aggressive approach, doing more to keep food safe and communi-
cating more clearly with the public when outbreaks occur.*

Once you've made the decision to encase a few men in a
metal pod and shoot the vessel into space, what you
don't want is to have something they eat make them sick. Astronauts in space already have suppressed immune systems,
and the added complications of food poisoning and its atten-
dant symptoms—dehydration, diarrhea—when both water

and privacy are limited likely goes without saying. That's why, in the late 1950s, just as NASA was embarking on the era of manned space flight, the agency went to its food supplier, Pillsbury, with a request: ensure that the food we're feeding astronauts won't have enough bacteria and other contaminants to make our astronauts sick. Pillsbury came through, crafting a science-based system that, for the first time, examined step-by-step how food was made, rather than the final product, with a focus on the riskiest ingredients and processes. By 1959, the problem of food-sickened astronauts was effectively kicked.

Back here on the ground, though, it's still 1958.

As things stand in the United States, food producers do very little to keep bacteria, as well as other common food contaminants such as viruses and chemicals, in check. Dr. Marion Nestle is a New York University food specialist who has worked with the Food and Drug Administration [FDA] to create food policy. "Right now, we don't have a food safety system," she tells *Science Progress*. But that is poised to change. This spring [2009], the House of Representatives passed a plan to finally apply the same sort of risk-based strategy to our food supply as NASA uses for astronauts. (The legislative vehicle in the House is H.R. 2749, the *Food Safety Enhancement Act*.) The Senate is set to take up the debate in the next few weeks.

---

*The mind-blowing truth is that the FDA today inspects food facilities somewhere on the order of once a decade.*

---

The fact is, there's a crying need for some sort of strategic intervention. Odds are that you have a few unpleasant memories of eating something that made you sick—according to the Centers for Disease Control [CDC], 76 million Americans get sick from food each year, some 325,000 of whom end up in the hospital. "These are way more than tummy aches," says Bill Marler, a Seattle attorney who specializes in food outbreak cases. During the infamous 1993 Jack in the Box outbreak, Marler represented a seven-year-old girl who spent 42 days in a coma. Once she came out of it, she had to learn to walk again. Then there are the 5,000 or so Americans who actually die each year from something they ate. People like Kyle Allgood, a two-year-old Utah boy whose mother fed him shakes blended with spinach in a bid to slip something healthy into his diet. The spinach, alas, was infected with a mutant strain of *E. Coli* known as 0157:H7. Kyle's kidneys were under attack, and proved outmatched.

## Safe Food for the Rest of Us

The genius of the Hazard Analysis and Critical Control Points [HACCP] system, as NASA's approach is known, is that it forgoes the myth that all foods are created equal and all food processing is equally risky. Vegetables often eaten raw, like the spinach Kyle Allgood ate, deserve to be tracked with a closer eye than produce that is, in common practice, heated to a kill point before it gets to the table. Fruits that producers cut into on the farm are also a risk—for instance in operations where harvesting and processing happen in the same space. The HACCP plan takes what science knows about what makes certain foods and certain processes a risk and uses our limited food safety resources to zero in on those weak points in the system. With those points identified, the Food and Drug Administration can, finally, come up with a plan that directs its attention where it is most needed. The mind-blowing truth is that the FDA today inspects food facilities somewhere on the order of once a decade. Under the bill currently [2009] up for debate in Congress, low-risk facilities would see that rate increase to one visit every year and a half to three years. Higher-risk facilities would be inspected every six to twelve months.

There are a number of other provisions in the plan that aim to do one simple thing: give us more knowledge about where what we eat is coming from. As things stand, our dinner plates are really black holes of information. Where did that tomato come from? That avocado? That grated cheddar cheese? The truth is that that information is so scattered, so hard to find, that it very nearly doesn't exist. No more, should advocates in Congress get their way. If the plan does pass, food will have a history. Under new traceability provisions, anyone who produces food in the United States will have to keep records of where the food came from before it got to them, and where it went when it left their shop. (There are exemptions for small farmers and direct-to-consumer operations like farm stands. More on that below.) Big operations will have to keep those records electronically, which is enormously helpful as public health officials start to look for patterns when outbreaks occur. And food facilities will—amazingly, for the first time—get unique identification numbers, so we know who's who.

Fairly simple changes, but a significant enough shift from the current state-of-play to be revolutionary.

Because the fact of the matter is that *not* knowing where what we eat comes from causes all sorts of problems, particularly in a day and age where we might be eating a West Coast cucumber, East Coast corn, and soybeans from China all in the same meal. (Food importers will have to abide by many of the same requirements as domestic food operations.) To be fair, part of the challenge is that nature makes it tough to track exactly what of what we've eaten is making us ill. Common food-borne bacteria—*E. Coli, Listeria, Salmonella*—incubate for up to a few days. Donna Rosenbaum started Safe Tables Our Priority, or S.T.O.P., after her seven-year-old daughter's best friend was the first life claimed during the '93 Jack in the Box outbreak. "What you're throwing up today isn't what made you sick," she explains. But the bigger problem is that knowing so little about where and how our food was made means that, when coupled with a distributed food supply, what could be limited eruptions of food poisoning turn into full-blown outbreaks and public health debacles. In one 2007 case, more than 1,300 people in 43 U.S. states got sick from a strain of *Salmonella*. Researchers soon found that all had eaten fresh salsa. Beyond that, though, mystery and confusion reigned. First jalapeño peppers became the scapegoat. Then tomatoes.

---

*Better data ... would give public health officials a fighting chance at detecting and stopping outbreaks at their front end, rather than resort to simply cleaning up a mess once it has gotten out of hand.*

---

Said Colorado Democrat Rep. Dianna DeGette during one congressional hearing, in a statement that would be comic if not for the thousand-plus people who suffered from the outbreak, "We could never really figure out what's wrong with the salsa."

"If you had better data," says Bill Marler, "you could say 'It's from this lot from this day and this facility,' rather than, 'We're recalling all the tomatoes.'" That confusion brings tragedy. In Kyle Allgood's sad case, the FDA knew for days that something was making people sick, but lacked enough information to pinpoint the particular cause and ask producers to pull their spinach from the market. Under current law, food recalls are all voluntary. Under the new plan, the FDA would be newly empowered to order a recall when conditions warrant.

Better data, especially in electronic form, would give public health officials a fighting chance at detecting and stopping outbreaks at their front end, rather than resort to simply cleaning up a mess once it has gotten out of hand. The plan before Congress would direct the CDC to develop a new epidemiological surveillance system that scours the data for signs of troubles in the food supply. What's more, the public would be given access to generalized sets of that data. The Reverend

Henry Whitehead, a medical amateur, played a role in determining how cholera works when he used publicly available data to track it back to its source during London's late-19th-century cholera outbreak. Who's to say that, with food data posted online, one of us might not help to spot and stop an outbreak before it spirals out of control?

## Seasoning a Plan for the National Appetite

By anyone's measure, government officials, especially those in the FDA and CDC, would be given considerable new power. When it comes to food safety, there will be more officials with more fingers in more pies, and that has some people worried. When Congress was considering H.R. 2749, there was an explosion of interest in the bill in the sustainable food movement, with a particular worry over how it would impact small farmers and farmers markets—exactly the sort of personal, people-centered food production and distribution many of us would like to see flourish.

And then there was the response on the political right, where the bill was read as an attempt by the federal government to wrap its hands around the American food supply, a particular sensitivity for those who prefer small government. (References to H.R. 2749 as the "Hitler Act" aren't even the most heated thing you'll read about it if you spend time on conservative blogs.) On the political right, what causes the most ire was the ID numbers for food facilities and the bill's "traceability" requirements—which shares many of the same outlines as the National Animal Identification System, now voluntary, which some worry might shift into a mandatory livestock tracking program.

But for food safety advocates, the concerns with the new plan, and the Internet clamor that accompanied them, are misguided and overblown. Negotiations in the House dropped the annual per-facility registration fee from $1,000 down to $500 in deference to representatives from coastal farm states worried that the cost—an attempt to provide FDA with a steady pool of funding to pay for increased inspections—would simply be too burdensome for the small local cheese maker or family farm. Some small producers, particularly those who deal directly with consumers, are exempt from many of the plan's more demanding requirements.

---

*Our current reactionary food system hurts farmers, big and small alike, and has a demonstrably negative impact on the ability of those who make food to live off their labors.*

---

That said, those who have been tracking and bemoaning the rate at which American foods make Americans sick don't see small size as a justification for not producing safe food. "Whether or not Kraft should meet the same standard as somebody who produces 20 pounds of cheese for their neighbors is one question," says Rosenbaum, "but if you're capable of producing a product that can kill someone, then you have to be on the lookout for that." She cites so-called "bathtub cheese." A delicacy in Latino communities in the United States, the homemade cheese also has a history of carrying dangerous levels of *Listeria*, and has been known to cause spontaneous abortions in pregnant women. When it comes to focusing on risky ingredients and risky ways of making food, "I can't think of any reason why small farmers should be exempt from doing this," says Nestle.

As for fears from the right that a risk-based food safety plan is Congress's back door into a mandatory animal-tracking future, the truth is that thanks to the might of the agriculture industry and Congress's weakness in the face of it, the plan stops well short of keeping tabs on every cow in America. In the United States, meat is the purview of U.S. Department of Agriculture, and the plan now before Congress limits itself to the Food and Drug Administration's areas of oversight.

Concerns from the right, left, and middle need to take into account the fact that our current reactionary food system *hurts* farmers, big and small alike, and has a demonstrably negative impact on the ability of those who make food to live off their labors. When we can't manage to figure out, as De-Gette put it, "what's wrong with the salsa," everyone who grows or produces something that goes into the salsa suffers. When peanuts are making people sick, as we saw in this spring's *Salmonella* bacteria outbreak that was eventually traced back to two peanut processing plants in Georgia and Texas, wary consumers swear off all peanuts, not just those that are actually no good. Produce rots in the fields. Good producers suffer. In the '07 salsa outbreak, tomatoes were ultimately cleared, within the margin of reasonable doubt, with having anything to do with the *Salmonella* contamination. That was little consolation for the U.S. tomato industry, which lost an estimated $100 million as the situation dragged out for six long and destructive weeks.

With better data, government health officials are given better odds at detecting an outbreak early, isolating the cause, and issuing warnings that actually eliminate the threat without causing collateral damage on innocent producers. And what has happened in the past is that government safety officials, burned by having reacted slowly to outbreaks in the absence of solid information, drag their feet on lifting warnings once the actual health threat has passed—meaning that our reactions to dangerous foods in the United States now carry the double-whammy of both being too late for consumers and going on too long for producers. When bad food is making people sick, the goal, says Bill Marler, "is to hold the people responsible who are actually responsible"—both perfectly sensible and a sea change from how we currently do things.

## A Fresh Start for the FDA

Whether the plan, if it indeed passes the Senate as expected, manages to target food safety risks while allowing small producers to flourish and food producers of all sizes to thrive free from too much government involvement depends in large part on the Food and Drug Administration. The FDA's track record when it comes to being smart about making food safe is, by general consensus in and out of the agency, decidedly mixed. But there are hopeful signs. Just last week, the agency opened the doors on a new online Reportable Food Registry where producers can quickly inform FDA when a case of food contamination crops up. And new administrators appointed by the [President Barack] Obama administration are pushing to make the agency more transparent and engage the public in its work. During this spring's *Salmonella* peanut outbreak, for example, the FDA reaction reflected a more aggressive and considered approach, using its website to post as much as it knew about what was making people sick, in as timely a way as possible, including pointing out what outside scientific experts had to say.

The hope is that by calling on the FDA to use what NASA and others have figured out about managing food risks, and by providing them with the resources necessary to actually put that knowledge to use, we can shrink the number of outbreaks that occur, spot them when they happen, limit the damage they do, and return business back to normal as quickly as possible. It's too late for Kyle Allgood and the many thousands of other Americans killed or seriously injured by what they ate. But we owe it to them to use the best of what science knows to give the rest of us a fighting chance.

# Local Farmers Need Protection from Excessive Regulation

*Lynn Byczynski*

*Lynn Byczynski is the editor and publisher of* Growing for Market, *a monthly journal and website resource for direct-market farmers. She is the author of several books, including* Market Farming Success, *published in 2006.*

*Wary consumers have increasingly turned to locally grown produce in light of food contamination outbreaks. But food safety legislation proposed in Congress places an unfair regulatory hardship on small farmers in not recognizing the differences between large and small scale farming operations. This has proven alarming to local small farmers who worry the extra cost and time of additional regulations will make it more difficult to stay in business. Provisions to account for these factors would help small farmers maintain high food safety standards and remain financially solvent as well.*

When the spinach contamination epidemic was happening in the fall of 2006, and supermarkets were pulling spinach from their shelves under order from the FDA [Food and Drug Administration] many local produce growers experienced a sharp increase in sales. Customers didn't stop eating spinach and other leafy greens—instead, many went to their farmers' market to buy local.

Lynn Byczynski, "Protecting Local Farms," *Yes Magazine*, September 17, 2009. Reproduced by permission.

"I was guessing it was going to really hurt us, but it was the complete opposite," said Pete Johnson of Pete's Greens in Craftsbury, Vermont, one of many growers who reported their sales went up or held steady during the E. coli scare. "People used it as a reason to not buy the California stuff. We sold double the usual amount of spinach for a couple of weeks there."

As the local food trend has gained momentum in recent years, it has become apparent that consumers want local food not just because it's fresher and tastes better, but because they believe it's safer and more wholesome than industrial food.

And so it is ironic and disturbing to know that the federal government's current push to improve food safety could threaten the viability of America's small farms. Farmers are in danger of being overwhelmed by recordkeeping, fees, inspections, and infrastructure requirements—unless Congress, the USDA [United States Department of Agriculture], and the FDA pay attention to the least powerful (though most popular) members of our agriculture community: local farmers.

## Pending Regulatory Initiatives

Right now, [September 2009] food safety legislation and regulation are whirling around Washington. Here are the big three initiatives that are occurring simultaneously:

1. In Congress, the House passed HR 2749, the Food Safety Enhancement Act of 2009. This legislation gives the FDA much broader powers to inspect and regulate food facilities, including farms. The Senate legislation gives the FDA much broader powers to inspect and regulate food facilities, including farms. The Senate is expected to take up its version of the bill this fall.

2. The Food and Drug Administration has released draft "guidances" for growing and handling tomatoes, leafy greens, and melons to prevent microbial contamination. The FDA says its documents represent the agency's current thinking on a topic, and are not binding. However, FDA Commissioner Margaret A. Hamburg said the guidances "will be followed within two years by enforceable standards for fresh produce."

3. The USDA has scheduled hearings on a national Leafy Greens Marketing Agreement, which would establish strict national standards for growing and handling about 20 vegetables and herbs, including arugula, cabbage, chard, cilantro, endive, escarole, kale, lettuce, parsley, raddichio, salad mix, and spinach. Although the standards are technically "voluntary," any grower who wants to sell wholesale is likely to have to comply with them.

All of this activity has occurred during the current growing season, when farmers are busy harvesting and selling. Many have no idea what is coming at them, and won't have time to assess the proposals until winter. But small-farm advocacy groups are alarmed about the direction of these food safety initiatives.

## Small vs. Industrial Scale

The first problem is that these regulations sweep small, direct-market farms into the same category as industrial food processors like Dole Foods. Visualize the typical small farm, where a farmer cuts salad mix with scissors and carries it in a basket to her packing shed to wash and box up for the next morning's farmers' market, after taking a bag to the house for her family's dinner. Then think about California's vast acreages of lettuce—harvested by machines, trucked to a factory for washing, cutting, and packaging, put on another truck and shipped to a warehouse, then to a supermarket, where it sits on a shelf until the expiration date arrives.

The small farmer would argue that her salad mix is not even the same product as the bagged supermarket stuff, known in the industry as "fresh cut." Production at such a large, industrial scale introduces risks that aren't present at the local level, such as contaminants introduced by machinery and packaging, or the increased risk of cross-contamination when produce comes from multiple farms. Yet the Leafy Greens Marketing Agreement calls for burdensome regulation of all leafy greens,

## Regulatory Burdens

The second big problem with the regulatory approaches to food safety is that they don't accommodate differences in scale. They require a significant amount of recordkeeping for all growers and handlers, a burden that will make life harder for already overworked and underpaid vegetable farmers. Small, diversified growers may have dozens of crops in the field each year, many of them only a few hundred plants, but they would be required to conduct the same intensive record-keeping as the corporation with hundreds of acres of a single crop.

The federal legislation, as passed by the House, exempts direct-market farmers who sell fresh produce. But if those farmers process their produce into a value-added product such as jams, salsas, or soup mixes, and sell more than 50 percent of their products wholesale, they will be required to pay the same fees and maintain the same records as, say, a potato chip factory. That provision is troubling to the National Sustainable Agriculture Coalition, which says it's unfair to charge a farm with $1,000 in value-added sales the same fees as one with $100 million in sales. Furthermore, small farms have to stay flexible about where they sell products, seizing whatever opportunities are open to them. The amount of produce they sell wholesale may fluctuate from one year to the next, creating a headache for both farmers and regulators.

One of the most troubling aspects of the food safety initiative is the frequent mention of keeping wildlife out of farm fields. In California, where growers are already required to meet the terms of that state's leafy greens marketing agreement, environmentalists are complaining that farmers are plowing grassed waterways and bulldozing riparian areas in an effort to deprive wildlife of habitat near their fields. They are erecting enormous fences to keep wildlife out of fields. Even if sustainable farmers agreed with this approach—and few do—it would be extremely expensive to keep wildlife out of production fields.

---

*No one is more concerned about food safety than local farmers.*

---

Growers are also apprehensive about testing requirements proposed by the various food safety regulations. Water, produce, maybe even seeds and soil amendments would have to be constantly tested for the presence of pathogenic microorganisms.

Growers in California have said that it costs them an average of $18,000 a year to comply with the state's leafy greens marketing agreement. Needless to say, that's beyond the means of most small-scale farmers.

## A Better Solution

No one is more concerned about food safety than local farmers. They are not selling to some distant, faceless public but to people they know—their customers come to their farmers' market booth every week, or pick up a regular share of food at their farm. Farmers who sell to restaurants are likely to have their names on the menu. And, for the most part, small farmers eat the food they raise on the land where they live. Direct market farmers have a personal connection to their customers and a powerful incentive to make sure their food is clean and safe.

In fact, spending time and money complying with regulations designed for much larger growers makes it harder for small farms to focus on what they do best: maintaining a strong connection to their land, their produce, and their customers. Growers groups across the country are developing training and certification programs in Good Agricultural Practices—the same concepts that are used by corporate farms, but scaled down to be useful to small farms.

By supporting programs like these, the USDA and FDA are in a position to create a win-win situation for small farms and food safety. Small growers and beginning growers need to know the latest, research-based information about food safety and how to apply it to their own farms. Rather than asking small farmers to shoulder a disproportionate share of the costs of industrial-scale programs, the federal government should increase funding to programs that will make sure every farmer has access to the information and tools that will keep food safe and maintain the momentum of the local food movement.

# 5

# Congress Must Reform America's Food Safety System

## Caroline Smith DeWaal

*Caroline Smith DeWaal is the Director of Food Safety for the Center for Science in the Public Interest (CSPI), a nonprofit health advocacy and education organization based in Washington, D.C. She often provides expert testimony on behalf of CSPI to Congress on issues of food safety. DeWaal co-authored the book* Is Our Food Safe?: A Consumer's Guide to Protecting Your Health and the Environment.

*The United States' food safety regulatory system is in urgent need of reform. The Food and Drug Administration [FDA] is the primary regulatory agency and it operates using aging laws and regulations that are not sufficient in addressing the complex nature of today's food production and delivery methods. Congress needs to act now to modernize the FDA and fund it sufficiently. The cost of inaction is high, both financially and in terms of illnesses and deaths Americans have endured during the numerous contaminated food outbreaks that have recently occurred.*

The American public cannot wait any longer for solutions to address a seriously broken food safety system. Successive outbreaks caused by numerous healthy foods like spinach, lettuce, tomatoes, peppers, alfalfa sprouts, and even such treats as ice cream and cookie dough have demonstrated that our hundred-year-old legal foundation and outdated strategies are inadequate to protect our citizens.

Reform of the food safety system is overdue. CDC [Centers for Disease Control and Prevention] estimates that foodborne diseases cause 76 million illnesses, 325,000 hospitalizations and 5,000 deaths annually. Economists believe that these illnesses pose a huge burden to society, with estimates for emergency room visits, hospitalizations, and lost work ranging from 40 billion to well over 100 billion dollars annually. Even if these numbers were cut in half, they are still too high. These are illnesses and deaths that are largely preventable.

Foodborne illnesses are most severe for the elderly, the very young, pregnant women, and immunocompromised people, and some illnesses lead to chronic medical conditions. Unfortunately, some outbreaks cause consumers to stop buying healthy foods, a fact demonstrated by depressed spinach sales after the 2006 outbreak. Consumer confidence in the safety of food has declined in recent years due to the steady parade of outbreaks.

## An Out-of-Date Regulatory Structure

Outbreaks are the result of an antiquated legal system that ties the hands of FDA when seeking food safety information from plants and limits the effectiveness of the agency to enforce the laws. The FDA operates under a number of laws that are 50 to 100 years old: the Federal Food and Drug Act of 1906, which focused on dangerous chemical preservatives; the Federal Food, Drug, and Cosmetic Act of 1938, which addressed economic adulteration of food and provided authority to set food standards and inspect factories; and the Public Health Service Act of 1944, which gave the agency authority to prevent communicable diseases transmitted in food. Food additive and pesticides laws gave FDA additional authorities in the 1950s. None of these was designed to address microbial hazards or emerging technologies.

Within this legal structure, the agency has developed regulations to cope with the need for new oversight for modern hazards. In the 1990s, the agency adopted regulations that put seafood and juice industries under mandatory Hazard Analysis and Critical Control Point (HACCP) programs. After a long hiatus, the agency recently adopted a new regulation covering egg safety at the production level. But the agency's approach of developing regulations food-by-food is proving brutally inefficient to protect the public. By the time one food is covered, the next problem has already emerged.

## The Consequences of the Broken Food Safety System Fall on the Consumer

Those who really pay the price for the antiquated legal and regulatory system are the consumers who must rely on it daily. Let me tell you about one consumer, a member of Safe Tables Our Priority. Michael Thomas was 50 years old when he became a victim of tainted peanut butter. Michael loved peanut butter and had a spotless health history. A father of four and grandfather of 20, Michael was known for his love of peanut butter. It was so well known that his own father called to warn him when he heard media reports about a peanut butter recall. Unfortunately, Michael had already eaten some of the *Salmonella*-contaminated product—and the consequences were severe, leading to reactive arthritis.

Michael spent weeks in and out of emergency rooms, suffering from dehydration, stomach pains, and high blood pressure. His right eye hemorrhaged. He was treated for nervous system damage, and damage to his heart, eyes, intestines, shoulders, and arms. This previously healthy man spent over five months bedridden. And because he lacked insurance at the time, he spent thousands on medical bills and lost his house due to the financial toll of his illness.

But Michael was lucky enough to survive, only to be shocked and outraged when it happened all over again this year. Michael was a victim of the *2007* tainted peanut butter outbreak, but when he heard of the 2009 outbreak—which sickened hundreds and killed at least nine people—he couldn't believe it. In a 2009 letter describing his experience with food-borne illness, Michael says, "I did take some comfort in the belief after it happened to me that the system was fixed and would not happen to any more families ... but here we are once again, literally right down the road from that very same plant I was poisoned from, with exactly the same situation, but even more widespread than it was before."

---

*The stories of outbreaks and recalls over the last few years are tragic, and they have had a huge impact on consumer confidence in the safety of the food supply.*

---

Just as Michael's 2007 experience was revisited in 2009, there is no question it will happen again—this year or next, from this product or another. Consumers will continue to be unwilling victims, until the system is fixed.

## The Public Is Ready for Congress to Address Food Safety

The stories of outbreaks and recalls over the last few years are tragic, and they have had a huge impact on consumer confidence in the safety of the food supply. But there is good news too. This is an area where the public understands that government plays a vital role in protecting them and their families.

In a poll on Americans' Attitudes on Food Safety [July 2009], commissioned by The Pew Charitable Trusts and conducted by Hart Research/Public Opinion Strategies, nine out of 10 American voters support the federal government adopting new safety measures, including the following individual measures:

- 92% support requiring *foreign countries* that export to the U.S. to certify that their food safety systems are as strong as ours

- 94% support requiring *tracing systems* that enable the FDA to trace food back to its source

- 91% support annual or semi-annual government *inspections of facilities* that process food that is at a high risk of contamination, including 75 percent who strongly favor this

- 92% support requiring food companies to *test for contamination and report* results to the government

- 90% support requiring *produce growers to meet standards* for water quality, manure use, and worker sanitation

- 89% support giving the FDA authority to issue *mandatory food recalls*

Since 2007, Congress has conducted 28 oversight and legislative hearings on food safety. These hearings often discussed the painstaking investigations by members of Congress and their staff of diverse outbreaks such as spinach tainted with *E. coli* O157:H7, peanut butter contaminated with *Salmonella*, and pet food adulterated with melamine. In every case, the hearings revealed flaws both in the food manufacturers' processes and in the Food and Drug Administration's oversight. With evidence of both unintentional and intentional contamination leading to large-scale outbreaks, it is little wonder the Government Accountability Office has highlighted the inadequate state of our food regulatory system and placed food safety in its high risk category three years in a row.

The evidence that FDA reform is needed has been made crystal clear in Congressional hearings, victims' stories, and voter polling. In addition, I think you will hear today that there is widespread consensus among a broad range of stakeholders that the time for passing this reform is now.

## Safety Must Be Built into the Food Supply System

The heart of any effective reform effort lies in prevention, not reaction. Congress should require every food processor regulated by FDA to have a food safety plan detailing that it has analyzed its operations, identified potential hazards, and is taking steps to minimize or prevent contamination. These hazard analysis and preventive control plans are already required for all meat and poultry plants, and such plans should be a prerequisite for all food processors that want to sell food in the U.S.

Prevention is our first line of defense when it comes to food safety. The Senate legislation establishes the industry's fundamental responsibility for ensuring food safety and provides a foundation for government inspections. However, the history of these programs where they have been implemented by FDA, such as in the seafood area, demonstrates that Congress must also give FDA the authority and funding to enforce compliance through regular inspections and access to company records.

---

*It is rare to see the level of consensus reflected among such diverse consumer and industry organizations on the need to fix our national food safety system.*

---

Additionally, FDA needs the authority to set performance standards for the most hazardous pathogens and to require food processors to meet those standards. The standards are used to ensure that food is produced in a manner that limits the likelihood of contamination by pathogens, chemicals, or physical hazards. Most importantly, performance standards set a level-playing field for the industry. Companies know in advance what standards will be enforced for their industry and products.

With mandatory food-safety planning combined with performance standards, the government can focus on more effective government oversight through frequent inspections, with analysis of records and laboratory test results. . . .

## The FDA Must Have Access to Producers' Records

I would like to highlight that FDA and state inspectors are also hampered in conducting inspections by restricted access to plant records that could help identify problems before they erupt into an outbreak. . . . FDA had to invoke the Bioterrorism Act to obtain records from Peanut Corporation of America of 12 tests that were positive for *Salmonella* in the year and a half leading up to the outbreak. Food Companies can refuse to disclose records to inspectors unless the FDA has a reasonable belief the food is adulterated, presents a risk of serious adverse health consequences or death, and the inspector presents a written demand. We saw this same situation play out in the 2007 Peter Pan peanut butter outbreak where, had inspectors been given access to test records, they would have been alerted to the plant's test results for *Salmonella*. To fix this, the law needs to be changed so that inspectors can access records that may allow them to prevent outbreaks. Meanwhile, the ability to access all food safety documentation during inspections is an essential tool to verify that control systems are present, maintained and operating properly.

## The FDA Food Safety Modernization Act

Both the House-passed bill and the one under consideration in this Committee share many similarities: processors must re-register periodically, implement food safety plans, meet performance standards, and administer programs to verify the food they import complies with U.S. law. In addition, FDA must conduct risk-based inspections and can require high-risk imported food to be certified as complying with U.S. law. Lastly, FDA can order a recall of food likely to cause serious illness or death.

Now is the time for Congress to fundamentally reform our food safety system. The year is fast drawing to a close, but enactment by the end of this year should be the goal. Two years ago, Congress expressed its commitment to adopt a modern regulatory oversight program at FDA and fund it adequately to fulfill its mission. Congress has increased the FDA food budget by 50 percent in that period, which lays the groundwork for this legislation. Bipartisan legislation has already passed the House of Representatives. . . . It is rare to see the level of consensus reflected among such diverse consumer and industry organizations on the need to fix our national food safety system. The public debate has defined the issues and we have a consensus for action. Congress can, with simple changes, take action this year to make food safer for American consumers. I urge you to act. There is no reason to delay.

# 6

# Imported Food More Likely to Be Contaminated than Food Grown in U.S.

*E.J. Mundell*

*E.J. Mundell is a journalist and managing editor for* Consumer News, *supplying comprehensive health news articles for publication to clients including the news media, governmental entities, and private or nonprofit organizations such as hospitals and health clinics.*

*Imported foods now account for 13 percent of Americans' diets. The lack of a well-funded inspection process makes the consumption of these foods far riskier than domestic choices. Highly publicized pet food contamination cases have highlighted significant challenges within China's quality oversight process, and have led to calls from other governments to enact stricter standards. But China is just one country struggling with this issue. The United States needs to enact stronger controls on imported foods from all sources and implement food traceability regulations so that when outbreaks do occur the source can be quickly pinpointed.*

One Sunday after church, Rich Miller headed to a local Chi-Chi's restaurant in Beaver, Pa., where he dipped into the house salsa that came with the meal.

That simple act in 2003 changed his life forever. What Miller didn't know was that imported Mexican green onions in the salsa carried a deadly passenger: hepatitis A.

E.J. Mundell, "U.S. Food Safety: The Import Alarm Keeps Sounding" *U.S. News & World Report,* January 15, 2008. Copyright © 2008 by U.S. News & World Report. Reproduced by permission.

A few days later, as Miller recalled recently, "I couldn't even get out of bed. It was like the worst case of flu that you could ever imagine."

His health quickly deteriorating, the 57-year-old railroad superintendent was diagnosed with rare fulminant hepatitis A disease—in which the virus destroys the liver—and was rushed to a Pittsburgh hospital for a liver transplant.

Placed in a medically induced coma for a month, Miller eventually returned home, frail and unable to return to work. To this day, he said, he has mobility problems and neurological difficulties.

Still, Miller considers himself lucky: Four others who ate the salsa and developed fulminant liver illness died. Overall, more than 600 people around Pittsburgh were sickened during what became the largest hepatitis A outbreak in U.S. history.

The story is just one of many over the past few years that have swung the spotlight on the dangers of imported foods, which now comprise 13 percent of the American diet, according to the U.S. Department of Agriculture.

## Imported Disasters

Perhaps the most high-profile examples of these potential dangers come from last year's tainted pet food scandal and the halting of questionable food products from China.

The pet food disaster, which slowly evolved into the largest recall of pet food in U.S. history, involved exported wheat gluten from China that contained the toxic chemical melamine and was used as an additive in food sold under more than 100 brand names. Hundreds of dogs and cats died; an official tally was never issued. In addition, U.S. health officials disclosed that up to 3 million broiler chickens had been fed the contaminated surplus pet food and then had been sold to restaurants and supermarkets across the country.

That was followed by a recall of almost a million tubes of toothpaste from China that were contaminated with a chemical used in antifreeze. The toothpaste had been distributed to institutions for the mentally ill, hospitals and prisons in the South.

And, shortly after that, U.S. health officials halted the importation of farmed fish from China because of chemical contamination in the fish feed.

*In November [2007], officials at the U.S. Food and Drug Administration reacted to the newest outbreaks with a sweeping set of proposals dubbed the Food Protection Plan.*

But China is not alone in triggering American foodborne woes.

Last year [in 2007] also, a salmonella outbreak caused Dole Fresh Fruit Co. to recall roughly 6,104 cartons of imported cantaloupes from Costa Rica that were distributed to wholesalers in the eastern United States and Quebec. There were no reports of illness.

But in 2006, an outbreak of nonfatal scombroid fish poisoning linked to tuna steaks imported from Vietnam and Indonesia sickened 15 people in Louisiana and Tennessee. And a 2001 outbreak of salmonella in Mexican cantaloupes killed two people and sickened 25 others across 15 states.

In November [2007], officials at the U.S. Food and Drug Administration [FDA] reacted to the newest outbreaks with a sweeping set of proposals dubbed the Food Protection Plan. It calls for legislation that would give the agency broader powers (including mandatory food recall), heftier financing, and improved cooperation with producers, importers and foreign governments to stop tainted food at the source. The plan remains just that, however, pending Congressional action.

Still, "I think it's clearly a step forward," said Bill Hubbard, who spent 14 years as associate commissioner of the FDA before retiring in 2005. Hubbard, who is now an adviser for the Washington, D.C.-based consumer advocacy group Coalition for a Stronger FDA, said, "The plan is clearly an attempt to change the paradigm from 'inspect only at the border' to putting more of the responsibility elsewhere," especially at the source of production abroad.

"Put in place procedures where you say to the importer you need to be checking on your supplier, then the exporter in China is supposed to be looking at his supplier and then all the way back to the producer," Hubbard explained. "Everybody is checking on everybody and keeping records. And, in theory, that can work. But the FDA will need new statutory authority to oversee something like that, and resources."

The full scope of the problem remains unclear, however.

---

*Inspections by the FDA—either at the source of production or at the borders—can't keep up.*

---

Food safety experts stress that it's almost impossible to sort out whether the thousands of smaller food-linked disease outbreaks that occur each year in the United States are attributable to domestic or imported product. According to the U.S. Centers for Disease Control and Prevention [CDC] about 76 million eases of food-related illness are reported in the United States each year, including 5,000 deaths.

## More Contaminants in Imported Foods

One thing is clear: You're more likely to encounter contaminants in foods from abroad than those grown in the United States.

According to a FDA report released in 2003, pesticide violations were cited in 6.1 percent of imported foods sampled versus 2.4 percent of domestic products. And a report issued by the agency a few years earlier found traces of salmonella or the dysentery-linked bacteria *shigella* in 4 percent of imported fruits and vegetables versus 1.1 percent of domestic produce.

And there's more imported food in the nation's supermarkets than ever before. According to the CDC, food imports to the United States have almost doubled in the past decade, from $36 billion in 1997 to more than $70 billion in 2007.

Trouble is, inspections by the FDA—either at the source of production or at the borders—can't keep up. The agency is responsible for inspecting all imported foods with the exception of meat and egg products, which are covered by the Food Safety and Inspection Service, part of the U.S. Department of Agriculture.

Overall, "there's been an 81 percent drop [in FDA inspections] since 1972," noted Michael Doyle, director of the Center for Food Safety at the University of Georgia, in Griffin. "That's a huge reduction, and, at the same time, compared to 1972, we have a huge amount more of food imports."

In fact, the FDA's own data show that the number of inspectors at its Office of Regulatory Affairs dropped from 1,642 in 2003 to 1,389 in 2005—even as food imports rose from 9.3 million shipments per year to more than 13.8 million shipments annually.

The reason for the shortfall is simple, Doyle said: "Reduced budgets."

The bottom line, according to FDA figures, is that its inspectors now sample just 1.3 percent of all imported food shipments entering the country.

However, simply boosting the number of inspectors may not be the solution, said Michael Rogers, who helps oversee FDA foreign and domestic inspections as director of the FDA's division of field investigations.

## Increased Collaboration Is Key to Reform

"With more [money], certainly more inspections can be done," he said, "but that's not the panacea for total public heath protection." Instead, Rogers said, collaborating with business and foreign governments to help spot tainted food before it reaches this country, which is part of the Food Protection Plan, may be the most important step the agency can take.

Certainly, the agency currently performs relatively few on-site inspections of foreign farms and food processing plants.

The farm in Ojos Negros, Mexico, that was the source of the 2003 green onion contamination had never been inspected by U.S. authorities before the incident. And the FDA inspection that took place soon after the outbreak makes for chilling reading.

In their report, filed in December 2003, agency inspectors said they observed dirty runoff from the farm workers' windowless, mud-floored shacks and crude showers seeping directly onto fields where produce was grown. Photos of the site "show evidence of soiled diapers, soiled feminine hygiene products, and domestic waste" lying nearby, according to the report.

The growing fields were irrigated with water from a pond that was also a dumping ground for human sewage and animal manure. During processing, green onions typically passed through the hands of at least six workers, the FDA team said, and there was no evidence that workers were allowed time off for illness. While the firm purported to wash all onions in chlorinated water, it could produce no evidence to back that claim.

## The Problem with China

The Chi-Chi's outbreak has been just one of many, and, in 2007, the focus shifted from Mexico to China.

The pet food scandal, as well as a stream of toy and other recalls in 2007, spurred negotiations between U.S. officials and their counterparts in China, which exported $4.2 billion worth of food to America last year—much of it in the form of ubiquitous processed food ingredients such as wheat gluten or ascorbic acid.

While no major outbreaks of human foodborne illness tied to Chinese products have occurred recently, they're not unlikely in the future, Hubbard said. Much of the food in China that's destined for U.S. dinner tables is grown and processed by mom-and-pop producers with little or no oversight, he said.

"What they've got is this vast cottage industry of producers making this stuff. Sometimes you might have a producer making just five or six sacks of flour per week in the hinterlands of China," Hubbard said. "China experts tell me that the central government in Beijing has very little influence out in the countryside where this is made."

China has reacted recently to international pressure by signaling that it is ready to tighten food safety standards. In December, the United States and China signed an agreement that places new registration and inspection requirements on 10 food products exported by Chinese companies. The products include some preserved foods, pet foods and farm-raised fish, all of which have come under suspicion of being tainted.

Those types of market reactions may help fix things in countries of origin such as China, experts say, but weaknesses remain here at home.

Topping the list: a chronic underfunding of FDA inspection services, according to critics. "If you look at the [George W.] Bush Administration's fiscal year 2007 budget proposal, the Produce Safety and other food programs are going to be cut by $22.6 million from 2006 levels, and the staffing would be reduced by 105 full-time employees," Doyle noted.

One private industry food safety inspector, Ed Sherwin, said he doesn't blame management or workers at the FDA for what he considers to be poor oversight of imported foods.

"What I've found is that the federal inspectors from FDA and USDA are excellent in their work, but they are under-staffed and overworked," Sherwin testified at a special Congressional hearing on the issue in October. In the meantime, "profits take priority over food safety," Sherwin said. "Food service operators tend to rely on their suppliers to provide the products that best meet their needs at the lowest price. Operators don't care if the crabmeat is from Maryland or Malaysia, the grapes are from California or Chile."

## Lack of 'Traceability'

Inspections at the border and ports of entry can help spot trouble, but experts say the FDA currently has full-time inspectors in place at just 90 of the nation's 300 import points of entry.

*Imported food is often hard to track once it gets by port inspectors.*

Then there's what's known as "port shopping," where shoddy goods are moved from one port to the next until they can be slipped past inspectors.

"Importers know that if FDA only looks at 1 percent, then even if they get caught at port A, chances are they won't get caught at port B," Hubbard explained. "Or they'll sometimes use things like inland ports for seafood. Shippers will enter their food through Las Vegas, where's there's no [FDA] sea-food person, because it's an inland port."

Testifying at the congressional hearing, Caroline DeWaal, of the Center for Science in the Public Interest, said imported food is often hard to track once it gets by port inspectors. "For example, with produce, it can all go into the same ware-house," she said. As part of normal distribution, she added, "they can mix boxes, and produce from several different countries can be reshipped out again without any kind of labeling."

This lack of "traceability" can make it tough to uncover the source of an outbreak and can cause worried consumers to avoid all brands of a given food, severely affecting an entire industry.

That scenario unfolded in the early days of the 2006 U.S. spinach scare, experts noted, with consumers simply avoiding the leafy green altogether, regardless of where it was grown.

Finally, there's the problem of what everyone calls the FDA's lack of clout in punishing companies that import dangerous foods. The agency is allowed by law to recall dangerous pharmaceuticals, but it has no such power over potentially deadly foods. The new Food Protection Plan does include a provision calling for mandatory recall authority, but it remains to be seen if legislators will grant the agency those new powers.

Moves toward more thorough and frequent inspections offer little comfort to food-poisoning victims such as Miller, who reached an out-of-court settlement of his lawsuit against Chi-Chi's before the company went out of business in the United States in 2004.

Miller said his story should remind Americans just how close the link is between what's on their forks and what's in fields thousands of miles away.

"Disease knows no boundaries," he said. "I know that we are still going to have outbreaks—nothing is perfect, and you can't stop everything. But we have to lessen it, and lessen its impact."

7

# More Inspections and Better Labeling Needed to Avoid Chinese Scandals

*Food and Water Watch*

*Food and Water Watch is a nonprofit organization working with grassroots organizations around the world to create an economically and environmentally viable future.*

*Chinese agricultural exports to the United States and the rest of the world have skyrocketed in the last five years. So too have the rates of sickness and death related to tainted food from China. Other countries, including Canada and Australia, have reacted swiftly and decisively in dealing with Chinese import problems. But the U.S. is hampered by underfunded inspection agencies and trade agreements calling for the free exchange of goods between the two countries, often at the expense of consumer safety. It is hoped that upcoming new labeling requirements that require information regarding where an imported food originated will allow consumers to make more informed decisions before deciding what is on the menu for dinner.*

In the last year [March 2008–March 2009] thousands of people worldwide have fallen sick from eating unsafe food produced in China. Lax inspections abroad and at home mean that Chinese food producers have relied on dangerous additives, fertilizers and pesticides, leaving consumers to contend with the dangerous residue of China's unregulated food production system.

Food and Water Watch, "Chinese Imports," foodandwaterwatch.org, March 2009. Copyright © 2009 by Food & Water Watch. Reproduced by permission.

And consumers are growing weary of the neverending scandals surrounding imports from China, from tainted dog food, to cookies laced with melamine, to the rising incidence of avian flu. A cursory look at newspaper headlines from any given month reveals the gravity and ubiquity of food safety problems in China:

> JAKARTA (*The Jakarta Post*)—Ten of 28 food products imported from China contain the toxic substance melamine, laboratory tests by the Indonesian Consumers' Foundation and the University of Indonesia (UI) have revealed.

> BEIJING (*Reuters*)—The impact of bird flu and the economic slowdown may have cut China's poultry numbers by about a third or more in the last month, executives in the poultry feed industry said on Tuesday.

> BEIJING (*New York Times*)—Seventy residents of southern China have been sickened after eating pig organs contaminated with a banned metabolism accelerator, state media reported Monday, in the latest in a series of lapses that have stirred international concern about China's control over food safety.

> BEIJING (*New York Times*)—Since September, inspectors have found melamine contamination in the milk products of 22 Chinese companies believed to have sickened almost 300,000 children and killed six. The scandal prompted a global recall of products made with Chinese dairy ingredients.

As the headlines pour in, so do the imports from China—in unprecedented numbers. In the last five years, the value of agricultural imports from China to the United States has more than doubled. And between 2007 and 2008, the value of consumer-oriented agricultural imports like nuts, fruit juices and fresh vegetables increased more than 20 percent, from $2,000,000,000 to $2,500,000,000. Seafood imports stand at similar numbers. China currently produces more than a third of the world's fruits and vegetables and more than half of the world's pork.

But China's massive agricultural production and export of cheap food products comes at a price to food safety—and U.S. regulators are not up to the job of protecting consumers.

In the last year, the U.S. Food and Drug Administration [FDA] refused nearly 2,000 shipments of Chinese imports. In January 2009 alone, inspectors refused 174 Chinese products, including 30 that were believed to contain melamine—a widely used chemical additive in China that FDA disallows in all but trace amounts in food items sold in the United States.

On the face of it, FDA's refusal of Chinese imports should give consumers a measure of relief. But in reality, FDA only manages to inspect a tiny fraction of imported products, around one percent, meaning a far greater number of imports travel through the U.S. border and onto grocery shelves uninspected.

Severely underfunded and dangerously overburdened, FDA is woefully ill-equipped to take on the tasks assigned to the agency, which include monitoring the safety of products that make up 20 percent of the entire economy and an estimated 80 percent of the food Americans eat. Included in those numbers are around $5 billion worth of food imports from China, found in every aisle of our grocery stores.

While food imports surge, FDA has lost around 80 percent of its field inspection personnel, due largely to a decline in government funding over the last three decades. A subcommittee of the agency's own science advisory board called the FDA's inspection rates "appallingly low. . . At most, it inspects food manufacturers once every 10 years."

The report goes on to state that the "FDA's ability to provide its basic food system inspection, enforcement and rule-making functions is severely eroded, as is its ability to respond to outbreaks in a timely manner and to develop and keep pace with the new regulatory science."

## FDA in Reactive, Not Proactive Mode

Because FDA lacks the resources to effectively carry out safety inspections, the agency serves as a reactive regulator, often waiting for illness or death to strike before it begins an investigation or issues warnings and recalls.

In September of 2008, Canadian food inspectors issued a recall on Chinese-made "Koala's March" cookies when they were identified as containing unsafe levels of melamine.

---

*China's inspection process cannot guarantee that it can enforce U.S. food safety standards.*

---

A widely used chemical in animal feed and some human foods in China, melamine disingenuously gives food products the appearance of high protein levels, allowing watered-down dairy products, for example, to pass quality tests.

Two weeks after Canada issued a recall of the cookies, FDA was reluctant to make a similar stand even as pressure from the public and the media was mounting—and the cookies continued to sell in grocery stores across the country.

Eventually the Alabama Department of Agriculture took matters in their own hands and issued a public warning about the cookies.

Three weeks after the Canadian recall, during which time an unknown number of cookies were bought and eaten by consumers, FDA finally issued a recall.

As the many tainted-food scandals show, China's inspection process cannot guarantee that it can enforce U.S. food safety standards. The Chinese government has issued a public statement to this effect, stating, "as a developing country, China's current food and drug safety situation is not very satisfactory because supervision of food and drug safety started late, its foundation is weak so the supervision of food and drug safety is not easy."

In the last five years, an explosion of Chinese food imports to America has included tainted seafood, dog food, and processed foods and also scores of poisonous non-food articles, like toothpaste, children's toys and pharmaceuticals. The Chinese government has responded to these food safety problems with both resistance and promises of increased regulations, the most recent of which was the establishment of a government food safety commission. However, the enormity of China as food producer, including an estimated 900,000 individual food-processing plants, and the continued, rapid growth of the country's food production, indicate that much larger reforms are needed within China's regulatory structure to ensure food safety.

---

*Another powerful force is working against the regulation of Chinese imports—the World Trade Organization.*

---

Meanwhile, FDA inspectors lack the resources to pick up the slack, and as a result, dangerous imports flood in the country unchecked, putting consumers at risk. Increasing the funding to FDA and ramping up inspections are crucial steps to ensure that the food we eat is safe and wholesome.

However, another powerful force is working against the regulation of Chinese food imports—the World Trade Organization.

## Putting Trade Promotion Before Public Health

China joined the World Trade Organization [WTO] in 2001, welcomed by companies in the U.S. who envisioned a freer flow of American exports into China and the continued importation of cheap products to American consumers. The Office of the United States Trade Representatives [USTR] boasted to Congress in December 2008 that U.S. exports to China have increased 240 percent since 2001, lauding the new trade agreement with one small caveat for agricultural products.

"China remains among the least transparent and predictable of the world's major markets for agricultural products, largely because of selective intervention in the market by China's regulatory authorities," the report stated.

Here, USTR is concerned about regulations only insofar as they can at times be "capricious" and "bedevil" American traders attempting to capitalize on the enormous consumer market in China. Absent from the USTR report is any mention of the regulatory deficiencies in China that bedevil American consumers, who buy and consume Chinese imports everyday.

Robert B. Cassidy, a former government official in USTR, was quoted in the *Washington Post* in 2007 saying that "so many U.S. companies are directly or indirectly involved in China now, the commercial interest of the United States these days has become to allow imports to come in as quickly and smoothly as possible," which has resulted in the U.S. "kowtowing to China" despite continued problems with food safety.

China's food safety problems go beyond chemical adulterants in food processing, too. USDA reports, "Chinese fruits and vegetables often have high levels of pesticide residues, heavy metals and other contaminants. Water, soil, and air are dangerously polluted in many rural areas as a result of heavy industrialization and lax environmental regulation."

Imported produce has been shown to be three times more likely to contain the illness-causing bacteria *Salmonella* and *Shigella* than domestic produce. Additionally, FDA found that imported fruits and vegetables were two to four times as likely to have illegal levels of pesticide residues as domestic fruits and vegetables.

FDA lacks the capacity to effectively monitor the quality and safety of Chinese imports, which included $100 million of fresh fruits and vegetables in 2008 and around $1.5 billion worth of juices and processed fruits and vegetables. Likewise, FDA has done little to curtail imports of produce or Chinese dairy products, which are imported freely under the WTO trade agreement.

When it was revealed last year that Chinese-made baby formula laced with melamine was causing infant deaths, nine countries, including Canada and Australia, temporarily banned imports of Chinese dairy products, sending a clear message to China that its food safety problems will not be tolerated. Consumer groups in the U.S. unsuccessfully called on lawmakers to take similar measures.

Because of the WTO and the huge volume of trade between the U.S. and China, it is difficult for the U.S. to institute moratoriums, bans and even ramped-up inspections without invoking sanctions from the WTO, which views such measures as artificial trade barriers. Such barriers violate a driving force behind the WTO—the free flow of goods, no matter the cost to consumer safety. In this way, the WTO creates another obstacle between consumers and safe food.

---

*Consumers will have some new ways to control what they buy when new Country-of-Origin Labeling (COOL) requirements finally go into effect.*

---

As just one example, in March of this year, China complained to the WTO about the United States' ban on the importation of Chinese poultry, a measure the U.S. took on the grounds that Chinese poultry is produced in an unsafe manner. In response, China has claimed that the ban "violates the basic rules of the WTO," and the country continues to use its leverage under the trade agreement to compel the U.S. to reconsider the ban.

## Country-of-Origin Labeling

Consumers will have some new ways to control what they buy when new Country-of-Origin Labeling (COOL) requirements finally go into effect after years of delay. Under new COOL requirements, many food products, such as meat and produce, will display a country-of-origin label, giving consumers the opportunity to make more informed decisions about the food they buy.

Unfortunately, current COOL rules have been weakened by legislators under pressure from industry lobbyists, and the labeling requirements no longer apply to foods that have undergone any processing. So, while apples, frozen green beans and catfish will bear a country-of-origin label, food items like applesauce, frozen vegetable mixes and breaded catfish will not. Billions of dollars of Chinese imports will continue to be sold to consumers unlabeled.

While the new COOL labels will help consumers make better-informed decisions about some of the food they buy, they won't provide protection from many of the serious food safety problems that persist in China. This is the responsibility of FDA, to sheriff the wild west of food production. And there's scarcely anywhere wilder than China.

8

# Genetically Modified Foods May Cause Allergic Responses

*Jeffrey M. Smith*

*Jeffrey M. Smith is the author of two books on the risks of genetically modified (GM) foods.* Seeds of Deception: Exposing Industry and Government Lies about the Safety of the Genetically Engineered Foods You're Eating *and* Genetic Roulette: The Documented Health Risks of Genetically Engineered Foods *are considered groundbreaking works on the harmful effects of GM foods.*

*Rising levels of food allergies in the United States may be linked to the increase of genetically modified (GM) foods. Data on allergic reactions is difficult to collect as individuals must be exposed to a substance, often more than once, in order to determine if an allergy exists. But there is increasing evidence that at least one GM crop, soy, is linked to the soaring number of allergic reactions to products containing GM soy. The lack of mandatory labeling for GM foods in the United States leaves millions of Americans unaware of the risks within their diet. Without labeling, the only foods safe from GM contamination are organic foods, which are not permitted to contain GM components, or foods specifically labeled non-GM.*

The huge jump in childhood food allergies in the US is in the news often but most reports fail to consider a link to a recent radical change in America's diet. Beginning in 1996,

Jeffrey M. Smith, "Genetically Engineered Foods May Cause Rising Food Allergies," Institute for Responsible Technology, May 2007. Copyright © 2007 by Virago. Reproduced by permission by Time Warner Books UK.

bacteria, virus and other genes have been artificially inserted to the DNA of soy, corn, cottonseed and canola plants. These unlabeled genetically modified (GM) foods carry a risk of triggering life-threatening allergic reactions, and evidence collected over the past decade now suggests that they are contributing to higher allergy rates.

## Food Safety Tests Are Inadequate to Protect Public Health

Scientists have long known that GM crops might cause allergies. But there are no tests to prove in advance that a GM crop is safe. That's because people aren't usually allergic to a food until they have eaten it several times. "The only definitive test for allergies," according to former FDA [Food and Drug Administration] microbiologist Louis Pribyl, "is human consumption by affected peoples, which can have ethical considerations." And it is the ethical considerations of feeding unlabeled, high-risk GM crops to unknowing consumers that has many people up in arms.

The UK [United Kingdom] is one of the few countries that conducts a yearly evaluation of food allergies. In March 1999, researchers at the York Laboratory were alarmed to discover that reactions to soy had skyrocketed by 50% over the previous year. Genetically modified soy had recently entered the UK from US [United States] imports and the soy used in the study was largely GM. John Graham, spokesman for the York laboratory, said, "We believe this raises serious new questions about the safety of GM foods."

Critics of GM foods often say that the US population is being used as guinea pigs in an experiment. But experiments have the benefit of controls and measurement. In this case, there is neither. GM food safety experts point out that even if a someone tried to collect data about allergic reactions to GM foods, they would not likely be successful. "The potential allergen is rarely identified. The number of allergy-related medical visis is not tabulated. Even repeated visits due to well-known allergens are not counted as part of any established surveillance system." Indeed, after the Canadian government announced in 2002 that they would "keep a careful eye on the health of Canadians" to see if GM foods had any adverse reactions, they abandoned their plans within a year, saying that such a study was too difficult.

## Genetic Engineering May Provoke Increased Allergies to Soy

The classical understanding of why a GM crop might create new allergies is that the imported genes produce a new protein, which has never before been present. The novel protein may trigger reactions. This was demonstrated in the mid 1990s when soybeans were outfitted with a gene from the Brazil nut. While the scientists had attempted to produce a healthier soybean, they ended up with a potentially deadly one. Blood tests from people who were allergic to Brazil nuts showed reactions to the beans. It was fortunately never put on the market.

*The only published human feeding study on GM foods ever conducted verified that portions of the gene inserted into GM soy ended up transferring into the DNA of human gut bacteria.*

The GM variety that is planted in 89% of US soy acres gets its foreign gene from bacteria (with parts of virus and petunia DNA as well). We don't know in advance if the protein produced by bacteria, which has never been part of the human food supply, will provoke a reaction. As a precaution, scientists compare this new protein with a database of proteins known to cause allergies. The database lists the proteins' amino acid sequences that have been shown to trigger immune responses. If the new GM protein is found to contain sequences that are found in the allergen database, according to criteria recommended by the World Health Organization (WHO) and others, the GM crop should either not be commercialized or additional testing should be done. Sections of the protein produced in GM soy are identical to known allergens, but the soybean was introduced before the WHO criteria were established and the recommended additional tests were not conducted.

If this protein in GM soybeans is causing allergies, then the situation may be made much worse by something called horizontal gene transfer (HGT). That's when genes spontaneously transfer from one species' DNA to another. While this happens often among bacteria, it is rare in plants and mammals. But the method used to construct and insert foreign genes into GM crops eliminates many of the natural barriers that stop HGT from occurring. Indeed, the only published human feeding study on GM foods ever conducted verified that portions of the gene inserted into GM soy ended up transferring into the DNA of human gut bacteria. Furthermore, the gene was stably integrated and it appeared to be producing its potentially allergenic protein. This means that years after people stop eating GM soy, they may still be exposed to its risky protein, which is being continuously produced within their intestines.

Although biotech advocates describe the process of genetic engineering as precise, in which genes—like Legos—cleanly snap into place, this is false. The process of creating a GM crop can produce massive changes in the natural functioning of the plant's DNA. Native genes can be mutated, deleted, permanently turned on or off, and hundreds may change their levels of protein expression. This collateral damage may result in increasing the levels of an existing allergen, or even producing a completely new, unknown allergen within the crop. Both appear to have happened in GM soy.

Levels of one known soy allergen, trypsin inhibitor, were up to 27% higher in raw GM soy. In addition, although cooking soybeans normally reduces the amount of this protein, the trypsin inhibitor in GM varieties appears to be more heat resistant. Levels in cooked GM soy were nearly as high as those found in raw soy, and up to seven times higher when compared to cooked non-GM soy. This suggests that this allergen in GM soy may be more likely to provoke reactions than when consumed in natural varieties.

Another study verified that GM soybeans contain a unique, unexpected protein, not found in non-GM soy controls. Moreover, scientist tested the protein and determined that it reacted with the antibody called IgE. This antibody in human blood plays a key role in a large proportion of allergic reactions, including those that involve life-threatening anaphylactic shock. The fact that the unique protein created by GM soy interacted with IgE suggests that it might also trigger allergies.

The same researchers measured the immune response of human subjects to soybeans using a skin-prick test—an evaluation used often by allergy doctors. Eight subjects showed a reaction to GM soy; but one of these did not also react to non-GM soy. Although the sample size is small, the implication that certain people react only to GM soy is huge, and might account for the increase in soy allergies in the UK.

## Increased Herbicides on GM Crops May Cause Reactions

By 2004, farmers used an estimated 86% more herbicide on GM soy fields compared to non-GM. The higher levels of herbicide residue in GM soy might cause health problems. In fact, many of the symptoms identified in the UK soy allergy study are among those related to glyphosate exposure. [The allergy study identified irritable bowel syndrome, digestion problems, chronic fatigue, headaches, lethargy, and skin complaints, including acne and eczema, all related to soy consumption. Symptoms of glyphosate exposure include nausea, headaches, lethargy, skin rashes, and burning or itchy skin. It is also possible that glyphosate's breakdown product AMPA, which accumulates in GM soybeans after each spray, might contribute to allergies.]

## GM Soy Is Linked to Several Health Conditions

If proteins survive longer in the digestive tract, they have more time to provoke an allergic reaction. Mice fed GM soy showed dramatically reduced levels of pancreatic enzymes. If protein-digesting enzymes are less available, then food proteins may last longer in the gut, allowing more time for an allergic reaction to take place. Such a reduction in protein digestion due to GM soy consumption could therefore promote allergic reactions to a wide range of proteins, not just to the soy. No human studies of protein digestion related to GM soy have been conducted.

There is at least one protein in natural soybeans that has cross-reactivity with peanut allergies. That means that for some people who are allergic to peanuts, consuming soybeans may trigger a reaction. While it is certainly possible that the unpredicted side effects from genetically engineering soybeans might increase the incidence of this cross-reactivity, it is unlikely that any research has been conducted to investigate this. GM soy was introduced into the US food supply in late 1996. We are left only to wonder whether this had an influence on the doubling of US peanut allergies from 1997 to 2002.

## Eating GM Foods Is Gambling with Our Health

The introduction of genetically engineered foods into our diet was done quietly and without the mandatory labeling that is required in most other industrialized countries. Without knowing that GM foods might increase the risk of allergies, and without knowing which foods contain GM ingredients, the biotech industry is gambling with our health for their profit. This risk is not lost on everyone. In fact, millions of shoppers are now seeking foods that are free from any GM ingredients. Ohio-based allergy specialist John Boyles, MD, says, "I used to test for soy allergies all the time, but now that soy is genetically engineered, it is so dangerous that I tell people never to eat it—unless it says organic."

Organic foods are not allowed to contain GM ingredients. Buying products that are certified organic or that say non-GMO are two ways to limit your family's risk from GM foods. Another is to avoid products containing any ingredients from the seven food crops that have been genetically engineered: soy, corn, cottonseed, canola, Hawaiian papaya and a little bit of zucchini and crook neck squash. This means avoiding soy lecithin in chocolate, corn syrup in candies, and cottonseed or canola oil in snack foods.

Fortunately, the Campaign for Healthier Eating in America will soon make your shopping easier. This Consumer Non-GMO Education Campaign is orchestrating the clean out of GM ingredients from foods and the natural products industry. The Campaign will circulate helpful non-GMO shopping guides to organic and natural food stores nationwide. The Campaign will provide consumers with regular GM food safety updates that explain the latest discoveries about why Healthy Eating Means No GMOs.

9

# Genetically Modified Foods Provide Safe and Healthy Choices for Consumers

*Agricultural Biotechnology Council*

*The Agricultural Biotechnology Council is the umbrella group for the agricultural biotechnology industry in the United Kingdom.*

*Products currently under development demonstrate that genetically modified (GM) crops can provide consumers with advantages beyond just lower cost. GM crops could potentially increase the health value of certain foods and protect fruits and vegetables from diseases that will lead to a larger supply of quality food from each harvest. Farmers should be allowed to choose what they grow while consumers must also have the freedom of choice when deciding what foods to feed their families.*

GM crops have been grown extensively around the world for the last 15 years, and two trillion meals with GM ingredients have been eaten with no substantiated evidence of harm to health. In 2009, over 14 million farmers in 25 different countries planted over 134 million hectares (around 300 million acres) of GM crops, including maize, soybeans, oilseed rape and even papayas; that is more than four times the land area of the British Isles. The question for people in the UK [United Kingdom] is: how does this help me?

Agricultural Biotechnology Council, "GM Crops and Consumers 2009," www.abcinfor mation.org, July 2009. By kind permission of the Agricultural Biotechnology Council.

## Consumer Benefits of GM Crops

To date, most GM crop production has addressed the productivity, availability and cost of food supplies, and hence has no clearly visible or easily identifiable consumer benefit. This is now changing, with specific consumer benefits close to market.

*Healthier oils and foods*

- Omega-3 fatty acids, commonly found in oily fish and widely known for their health benefits in helping to fight cardiovascular disease, are now contained within a GM soybeans currently under development. These soybeans will be processed into soya oil (often sold as "vegetable oil") and used to provide a range of foods with significant health benefits.

- A GM tomato supplemented with genes from snapdragon flowers (rich in an antioxidant called anthocyanin), developed by the John Innes Centre, could have cancer-fighting properties.

- Golden Rice, fortified with increased levels of pro-vitamin A, is now at the advanced field trial stage of development in the Philippines, and is now supported by the Gates Foundation.

- Researchers in Cambridge have produced a type of GM wheat that releases fewer calories into the body compared to other varieties currently available.

*The potential for allergy-free foods*

- Scientists have identified a new gene in peanuts that codes for a protein with no apparent allergic effects, research that opens up the possibility of allergen-free GM nuts.

*Food with a lower carbon footprint*

- In the UK [United Kingdom], agriculture accounts for 7% of all carbon emissions; the use of GM technology can help in reducing the carbon footprint and environmental impact of farming in a number of ways.

- GM crops can help decrease the need for ploughing, helping farmers adopt less intensive agricultural methods and so further reducing the carbon footprint of the food chain.

- GM crops are being developed that require 50% less fertiliser, a major part of the carbon footprint of a crop.

*Protecting fruits and vegetables from disease*

- In the UK, recent trials have been successfully undertaken of GM potatoes with intrinsic resistance to devastating diseases such as blight.

- Papayas genetically modified to resist Ringspot-Virus (a disease that can sharply lower yields) are being grown in the US and Canada, greatly increasing the quantity of papayas available for consumption and exported abroad, and saving one of Hawaii's major industries.

- Several international institutes are developing apples with resistance to dozens of different diseases including fire blight, apple scab, and powdery mildew. With conventional breeding the production of scab-resistant varieties of good eating quality and suitability for commercial production can take as long as 50 years.

## Consumer Attitudes to GM Foods

Consumer choice is about ensuring that people have the opportunity to buy the widest possible range of products according to their own tastes and requirements. That right to choose should include GM foods. Likewise, farmers should have the opportunity to grow GM crops along with organic and non-GM, so providing consumers with genuine choice and an ability to benefit from them if they so choose.

Much consumer attitude research fails to qualify a simple yes/no response by a level of relative importance. In contrast to many claims, the majority of consumers do not regard GM as a major concern despite attempts from those opposed to the technology to make it a polarised debate. This is highlighted by an EU report published last year, which showed that where GM is on the shelf, it sells; nevertheless, there remains a significant gap in consumer knowledge about how the technology works.

*Consumers are starting to recognise the benefits*

- An IGD [Institute of Grocery Distribution] report (2008) suggests that a majority of consumers do recognise that there are important potential benefits of GM crops.

- 52% of those polled believed that GM can be used to increase productivity and feed a growing world population, while only 13% disagreed.

- Additionally, 47% of consumers thought that GM can help to protect crops against disease and extreme weather.

*The majority of consumers remain undecided, but most are unconcerned*

- Research by the Food Standards Agency in 2009 suggests that UK consumers do not have a strong interest in GM: only 6% of those surveyed expressed unprompted concern about GM food.

- In summer 2008, after a high level of media coverage of the GM debate, IGD tested the level of support and opposition towards GM foods in the UK. The largest proportion of respondents (54%) neither supported nor opposed GM. A further 29% expressed a mild opinion and only 14% were strongly opposed to GM.

*However, there is still a lack of understanding about how the technology works*

- IGD tested the level of perceived knowledge of GM foods amongst consumers. Just under half (48%) believed that their knowledge was 'poor' or 'very poor'. Just 7% were able to give an accurate definition of GM.

Public discussion of GM is based on a low understanding of what it is, and deliberate attempts to cause confusion, which is restricting progress in understanding and opinion, and a failure to engage the public in a meaningful debate.

# 10

# School Lunch Programs Lag Behind Other Industries in Food Safety

*Elizabeth Weise and Peter Eisler*

*Elizabeth Weise is a science reporter for* USA Today. *Peter Eisler specializes in investigating health and environmental issues for* USA Today.

*The United States' National School Lunch Program does not have adequate systems in place to prevent students from being exposed to contaminated food products. Lunch program food safety has fallen behind other food based industries by focusing almost exclusively on price in order to provide school lunches for the lowest possible cost. But higher quality standards employed by other industries such as fast-food restaurants have proven that demanding more from suppliers does not necessarily mean increased expense. Given children's higher vulnerability to food-borne illnesses, a more significant question would be why are we willing to risk the health of our children in order to save a few dollars.*

As Congress and the Obama administration seek new ways to assure the safety of food served to the nation's schoolchildren, the most promising paths are no secret.

Scientists and food safety experts say there are industries and major companies, both in the United States and abroad, that have made great strides in safety and consistently produce food free of the bacteria that sicken about 75 million Americans a year. Can those practices become the rule for the food the government buys for schools?

## School Standards Fall Behind

It has been a decade since the U.S. Department of Agriculture [USDA] decided that the ground beef it buys for school lunches must meet higher safety standards than ground beef sold to the general public. But those rules, which required that school lunch meat be rejected if it contains certain pathogens, such as salmonella, have fallen behind the standards that fast-food chains and other businesses are adopting on their own.

Moreover, the special protections that the USDA sets for the ground beef it sends to schools do not extend to other products the federal government—or schools themselves—purchase for student meals. No extra testing is required for the spinach, the peanuts or the tortillas served in schools and, sometimes, those products present similar health risks.

Today, Agriculture Secretary Tom Vilsack has embraced a different measure for food safety—one that goes beyond pathogen tests and looks at the true toll: how many people get sick. "Until we get the number of food-borne illnesses down to zero, and the number of hospitalizations down to zero, and the number of deaths down to zero, we still have work to do," he said this fall [2009].

*The school lunch program could become the standard-bearer for food safety.*

The stakes are especially high for schoolchildren with still-developing immune systems. There were more than 470 outbreaks of food-borne illnesses in schools from 1998 through 2007, sickening at least 23,000 children, according to a *USA Today* analysis of data from the U.S. Centers for Disease Control and Prevention. Yet the USDA's National School Lunch

Program, which provides food to nearly every school district in the country, lacks systems to ensure that students don't get tainted products from poorly vetted suppliers, the newspaper found.

## Reform Is on the Way

Vilsack has pledged to address the problems, and members of Congress are vowing to do the same as they work to update the Child Nutrition Act, which governs the National School Lunch Program.

Congress has a responsibility "to make certain the foods provided to schools are the safest possible," says Sen. Saxby Chambliss, R-Ga., the senior Republican on the Senate agriculture committee.

Another committee member, Sen. Kirsten Gillibrand, D-N.Y., has introduced a bill requiring new initiatives to ensure that recalled products are removed quickly from school pantries. She and a House counterpart, Rep. Joe Sestak, D-Pa., also are pressing the USDA to stop using school lunch suppliers with poor safety records—and to set standards for school lunch food that mirror those used by fast-food chains and other discriminating companies.

The school lunch program could become the standard-bearer for food safety, says Carol Tucker-Foreman, who oversaw school lunch purchases as assistant undersecretary of the U.S. Department of Agriculture during the Carter administration. She says that instead of buying the cheapest possible food for schoolchildren, as it does now, the government could seek out suppliers that meet high standards and then let them advertise that they have USDA's seal of approval.

Companies could boast that "'We're qualified to sell to the school lunch program,'" says Tucker-Foreman, now senior fellow at the Consumer Federation of America's Food Policy Institute.

What lessons could the National School Lunch Program learn from the industries, companies and universities that have pioneered breakthroughs in food safety? Among those cited by experts:

*It is possible to produce safer food by raising standards without breaking the bank.*

McDonald's did it, after a brush with catastrophe.

In 1982, hamburgers from the fast-food chain sickened at least 47 people in Oregon and Michigan. No one died, but the pathogen that caused the severe cramps, abdominal pain and bloody diarrhea turned out to be a little-known, especially dangerous form of the common stomach bacteria E. coli. The new subtype, E. coli O157:H7, produced a toxin that destroyed red blood cells and, in later cases elsewhere, caused kidney failure or death.

## McDonald's Moves Ground Beef Safety Forward

Confounded by the discovery, McDonald's hired one of the nation's best-known food safety scientists, Michael Doyle, and told him, he recalls, "to bulletproof their system so E. coli never happened to them again."

McDonald's reconsidered its old assumptions about food— from how often beef-processing plants should test ground beef to how well a hamburger must be cooked to kill off pathogens such as E. coli and salmonella.

The results helped change the industry. For years, the federal food code said burgers had to be cooked only until their internal temperature reached 140 degrees; McDonald's tests showed the safe standard was 155 degrees and that the meat must register that temperature for at least 15 seconds.

Microbial data also altered the demands McDonald's imposed on its suppliers. After a couple of years, the company saw that "about 5% of the suppliers could not get down to what we considered a reasonable level for salmonella and E.

coli," says Doyle, now director of the University of Georgia's Center for Food Safety. "McDonald's worked hard with them, but they couldn't get there, so McDonald's let them go."

The standards have worked, by all accounts. Seattle-based based food safety lawyer Bill Marler, who has been involved in almost all the major food safety lawsuits of the past 15 years, says he hasn't sued McDonald's since 1994 for a company-based E. coli illness and can't think of anyone else who has.

---

*Organizations with greater buying power—such as fast-food chains or the school lunch program—can set higher standards, and industry ultimately will meet those standards because that's where the money is.*

---

Other fast-food chains, including Jack in the Box and Burger King, have adopted similar practices, *USA Today* found, and many have continued to toughen their standards. As a result, many of those companies now have sampling and testing requirements for ground beef that go beyond the standards USDA set for school lunches in 2000.

At that time, USDA officials feared that their demand for sampling and testing of school meat—and their move to a "zero tolerance" standard for salmonella and E. coli O157:H7— would drive away the program's suppliers, says Barry Carpenter, who spearheaded the new rules as an official with the USDA's Agricultural Marketing Service.

## Suppliers Meeting Stricter Standards

In the beginning, that's what happened: When the agency put its first orders out to bid in the months after the requirement was set, "we didn't get many bids, maybe not any, and the prices were high," says Carpenter, now head of the National Meat Association. "But eventually, one or two companies started bidding. Then, other companies realized, 'Oh, they're bidding at this price and they're making money,' and then we started getting more bids. . . . By fall (of 2000), we were getting an adequate supply at a reasonable price."

The lesson, many analysts say, is that organizations with great buying power—such as fast-food chains or the school lunch program—can set higher standards, and industry ultimately will meet those standards because that's where the money is. The school lunch program purchases huge volumes of commodities such as beef, poultry and other staples—$830 million worth in 2008.

"If you look at the school lunch business, it's a very big business," says Craig Wilson, assistant vice president for quality assurance and food safety at Costco, another company that imposes strict standards on its suppliers. "Could they improve and toughen their specs? Sure they could."

How much would it cost? David Theno, a safety specialist who overhauled Jack in the Box's safety practices in the 1990s, estimates the new requirements there added less than a penny a pound to its beef bills.

Higher food safety standards might not cost anything at all, says Helen Jensen, an agricultural economist at Iowa State University in Ames, Iowa. Buyers—at least those big enough to have any clout—often don't pay more for higher standards.

It's not that the buyer says, "'Here, I've added these extra tests, who wants to pay more for it?' It's more: 'These are the specifications for our product, (and) if you want to sell to us, this is who we'll buy from,'" Jensen says.

*You can go only so far with killing pathogens at the processing plant. Eventually, food safety has to reach back to the farm.*

European Union members focus on lowering levels of pathogens in animals before they are slaughtered. One much-cited example is Sweden, which has virtually eliminated salmonella in chicken and eggs by requiring the destruction of any flock that tests positive for the disease.

## U.S. Takes a Different Approach than E.U.

In the United States, the focus has instead been on technological solutions after the harvest—anti-microbial dips, disinfecting sprays and testing.

It's partly a matter of efficiency: There are millions of ranchers and thousands of feedlots where cattle are raised and fattened, but only 50 processing plants. So in terms of the cost-effectiveness of installing safety systems, "the packing plants made the most sense," says Mike Engler, president of Cactus Feeders, a feedlot in Amarillo, Texas. Engler, a biochemist, has chaired the National Cattlemen's Beef Association's beef safety committee.

Produce is different. In the United States, the safety drive recently has shifted to the field and farm—and is furthest along in leafy greens.

## Contaminated Spinach Leads to Drastic Produce Reform

Three and a half years ago, an E. coli O157:H7 outbreak tied to spinach from Earthbound Farm killed five people and sickened at least 205, setting off a nationwide recall. Since then, the company in particular and California and Arizona leafy greens growers in general have remade themselves.

Western Growers, which represents the California and Arizona produce industry, estimates that producers lost about $100 million in sales because of the spinach recall. Researchers at Rutgers University's Food Policy Institute found that a majority of consumers stopped buying spinach and that a fifth would not buy other bagged produce, either.

"Industry couldn't wait for the government" to solve the problem, says Wendy Fink-Weber, a spokeswoman for Western Growers. So the growers worked with universities, food safety experts and processors to write new standards that are overseen by the California Department of Food and Agriculture and paid for by the growers.

The standards require bacterial testing of irrigation water, named as a possible source of contamination in federal reports. If test results suggest a problem, the vegetables themselves are tested for E. coli O157:H7 and salmonella. If either is found, the crop cannot be used for human consumption.

"There's a huge cultural shift," says Hank Giclas, Western Growers' vice president for science and technology. So far, 120 California growers and handlers have voluntarily signed on to the standards. Arizona growers worked with their state officials to implement similar standards in September 2007.

## Further Safeguards Implemented and Faster Action Employed

Earthbound Farm went even further. The company, based in San Juan Bautista, Calif., also tests all seeds and fertilizers for E. coli O157:H7 and salmonella, then tests both raw and finished product and holds it until the tests come back negative; testing usually takes between 12 and 16 hours.

Will Daniels, Earthbound's vice president in charge of safety, says the new processes add about 3 cents to the cost of a package of baby greens.

California and Arizona together grow 90% of the leafy greens Americans eat, Fink-Weber says—which means that at least some schools already have salad bars operating under these high standards. Safety standards for produce could become even more important when Congress takes up reauthorization of the Child Nutrition Act because there's mounting pressure to emphasize fresh fruits and vegetables in schoolkids' diets.

A group of legislators, led by Rep. Sam Farr, D-Calif., is pushing a bill to require the USDA to increase produce purchases for schools' feeding programs and encourage use of salad bars in schools.

*Move faster when trouble erupts.*

When Costco learns that one of its suppliers has recalled a product, the members-only retailer does more than pull the item off its shelves. Because its shoppers swipe a customer identification card at checkout, Costco can track anyone who purchased the recalled product, and each of them gets an automated phone call informing them of the recall.

---

*Commodities purchased through the National School Lunch Program often pass through multiple processors and distributors, and there's no system for tracking specific foods to their final destination.*

---

The calls, up to 870,000 per hour, are made immediately after a recall is initiated, arriving in some cases before the official announcement is posted on government websites. And Costco follows up with a written letter to each affected household.

"If I have knowledge (of a recall), I better do something about it . . . beyond putting a sticker in the aisle," says Wilson, the company's safety chief.

## Schools Should Adopt More Technology, Experts Say

Costco's use of modern technology is the sort of approach that some experts believe the USDA should adopt when it comes to advising schools about recalls of school lunch products, whether those products were bought by the government or purchased directly by schools themselves.

Earlier this year, an audit by Congress' Government Accountability Office noted that both the USDA and the Food and Drug Administration [FDA] lack systems for giving schools timely alerts when products such as peanut butter—the focus of a nationwide recall this year—are bought for student meals.

Part of the problem is that commodities purchased through the National School Lunch Program often pass through multiple processors and distributors, and there's no system for tracking specific foods to their final destinations. That undermines efforts to "inform states and school districts which products were produced with recalled foods and which were not," the auditors reported.

In some cases, such problems have led unwitting school officials to serve recalled food, the auditors found, though they could not determine whether any students were sickened as a result.

Gillibrand's bill would require the FDA and the USDA to develop new systems for identifying whether foods implicated in a safety investigation may have been distributed to schools. It also would push the USDA to find ways to alert schools to recalls more quickly and effectively.

Improving the recall system is the first step the government should take to assure the safety of school lunches, says Dora Rivas, head of food and nutrition services for Dallas schools and president of the School Nutrition Association, which represents school meal directors. It is time, she adds, to "bring this system into the digital age."

# Organizations to Contact

*The editors have compiled the following list of organizations concerned with the issues debated in this book. The descriptions are derived from materials provided by the organizations. All have publications or information available for interested readers. The list was compiled on the date of publication of the present volume; the information provided here may change. Readers need to remember that many organizations take several weeks or longer to respond to inquiries.*

**American Council on Science and Health (ACSH)**
1995 Broadway, Second Floor, New York, NY   10023-5860
(212) 362-7044 • fax: (212) 362-4919
e-mail: acsh@acsh.org
website: www.acsh.org

ACSH provides consumers with scientific evaluations of food and the environment, pointing out both health hazards and benefits. It compiles the Health Facts and Fears at Riskometer .org, which attempts to put risk in perspective.

**Center for Consumer Freedom**
PO Box 34557, Washington, DC   20043
(202) 463-7112
website: www.consumerfreedom.com

The Center for Consumer Freedom is a nonprofit coalition supported by restaurants, food companies, and consumers working to promote personal responsibility and protect consumer choices. The Center opposes health care advocates, food advocates, and politicians who, it believes, are taking away Americans' freedom to eat and drink what they choose.

**Center for Food and Justice (CFJ)**
1600 Campus Road MS M-1, Los Angeles, CA   90041-3314

(323)341-5099 • fax: (323) 258-2917
e-mail: cfj@oxy.edu
website: http://departments.oxy.edu/uepi/cfj/

The Center for Food and Justice is a division of the Urban and Environmental Policy Institute at Occidental College. With its vision of a sustainable and socially just food system, CFJ engages in collaborative action strategies, community capacity-building, and research and education.

### Center for Global Food Issues (CGFI)

PO Box 202, Churchville, VA   24421-0202
(540) 337-6354 • fax: (540) 337-8593
website: www.cgfi.org

The Center for Global Food Issues researches and publishes articles about agriculture and the environmental concerns related to food and fiber production. The center supports genetic engineering, pesticide use, irradiation of food, and other uses of technology in agriculture.

### Center for Science in the Public Interest (CSPI)

1875 Connecticut Ave. NW, Suite 300, Washington, DC   20009
(202) 332-9110 • fax: (202) 265-4954
e-mail: cspi@cspinet.org
website: www.cspinet.org

The Center for Science in the Public Interest is a consumer advocacy organization whose twin missions are to conduct innovative research and advocacy programs in health and nutrition and to provide consumers with current, useful information about their health and well-being. CSPI supplies information to the public and policy makers and conducts research on food, alcohol, health, the environment, and other issues related to science and technology.

### Consumer Federation of America (CFA)

1620 I Street NW, Suite 200, Washington, DC   20006
(202)387-6121

e-mail: cfa@consumerfed.org
website: http://www.consumerfed.org

The Consumer Federation of America includes a division called The Food Policy Institute, which conducts research and engages in advocacy to promote a safer, healthier and more affordable food supply. The Institute supports continued reform of federal food safety programs, mandatory labeling for genetically engineered foods, and expanding and improving programs to reduce hunger.

### Environmental Working Group (EWG)

1436 U St. NW, Suite 100, Washington, DC   20009
(202) 667-6982
website: www.ewg.org

The Environmental Working Group is a nonprofit organization of scientists, engineers, policy experts, lawyers, and computer programmers who research threats to the environment and people's health and look for solutions to environmental problems. In addition, the group lobbies for stronger regulations on the environment.

### Food First

398 Sixtieth St., Oakland, CA   94618
(510) 654-4400 • fax: (510) 654-4551
e-mail: info@foodfirst.org
website: www.foodfirst.org

Food First is a member-supported, nonprofit progressive think tank and education center. Its goal is to find solutions to hunger and poverty around the world. Food First publishes books, reports, articles, and films, and provides a variety of lectures, workshops, and academic courses for the public and policy makers.

### Food Safety and Inspection Service (FSIS)

1400 Independence Ave. SW, Room 2932-S
Washington, DC   20250-3700

(402) 344-5000 • fax: (402) 344-5005
e-mail: fsis.webmaster@usda.gov
website: www.fsis.usda.gov

The Food Safety and Inspection Service is the public health agency of the U.S. Department of Agriculture responsible for ensuring that the nation's commercial supply of meat, poultry, and egg products is safe, wholesome, and correctly labeled and packaged. It publishes fact sheets, reports, articles, and brochures on food safety topics.

**Food Safety Consortium (FSC)**
110 Agriculture Building, University of Arkansas
Fayetteville, AR   72701
(479) 575-5647 • fax: (479) 575-7531
e-mail: dedmark@uark.edu
website: www.uark.edu/depts/fsc

Congress established the Food Safety Consortium, consisting of researchers from the University of Arkansas, Iowa State University, and Kansas State University, in 1988 through a special Cooperative State Research Service grant. It conducts extensive investigation into all areas of poultry, beef, and pork meat production. The consortium publishes the quarterly *FSC Newsletter*.

**Friends of the Earth (FOE)**
1100 15th Street NW, 11th Floor, Washington, DC   20005
(202) 783-7400 • fax: (202) 783-0444
e-mail: foe@foe.org
website: www.foe.org

Friends of the Earth monitors legislation and regulations that affect the environment. Its Healthy People initiative speaks out about emerging technologies and harmful chemicals found in consumer products and in our communities, and the potentially serious impacts on people and our environment. FOE publishes the quarterly *Friends of the Earth Newsmagazine* and monthly newsletters.

## Grocery Manufacturers Association (GMA)

1350 I Street NW, Suite 300, Washington, DC   20005
(202) 639-5900 • fax: (202) 639-5932
e-mail: info@gmaonline.org
website: www.gmaonline.org

The Grocery Manufacturers Association represents the world's largest food, beverage, and consumer product companies. GMA's goal is to ensure that the laws and regulations governing food marketing and production are feasible, practical and based on sound information. One of its core operating principles is to bolster consumer confidence in the food supply.

## Harvard Center for Risk Analysis (HCRA)

401 Park Drive, Boston, MA   02215
(617) 432-4343
e-mail: jkh@harvard.edu
website: www.hcra.harvard.edu

The Harvard Center for Risk Analysis is an organization of biotechnology companies, large food processors, and chemical, pesticide, and petroleum manufacturers. The center analyzes and evaluates the potential risks posed by agricultural and medical technology.

## Organic Consumers Association (OCA)

6771 South Silver Hill Drive, Finland, MN   55603
(218) 226-4164 • fax: (218) 353-7652
website: www.organicconsumers.org

The Organic Consumers Association is a nonprofit public interest organization that deals with issues of food safety, industrial agriculture, genetic engineering, corporate accountability, and environmental sustainability. The OCA is the only organization in the United States focused exclusively on representing the views and interests of the nation's estimated 10 million organic consumers.

## US Food and Drug Administration (FDA)
10903 New Hampshire Ave., Silver Spring, MD   20993-0002
(888) 463-6332
e-mail: webmail@oc.fda.gov
website: www.fda.gov

The FDA is a public health agency charged with protecting American consumers by enforcing the federal Food, Drug, and Cosmetic Act and several related public health laws. To carry out this mandate of consumer protection, the FDA has investigators and inspectors cover the country's almost ninety-five thousand FDA-regulated businesses. Its publications include government documents, reports, fact sheets, and press announcements.

## Weston A. Price Foundation
4200 Wisconsin Ave. NW, Washington, DC   20016
(202) 363-4394 • fax: (202) 363-4396
e-mail: info@westonaprice.org
website: www.westonaprice.org

The Weston A. Price Foundation is a nonprofit founded in 1999 to disseminate the research of nutrition pioneer Dr. Weston Price, whose studies of isolated nonindustrialized peoples established the parameters of human health and determined the optimum characteristics of human diets. The Foundation is dedicated to restoring nutrient-dense foods to the human diet through education, research, and activism.

# Bibliography

## Books

Wendell Berry

*Bringing It to the Table: On Farming and Food.* Berkeley, CA: Counterpoint, 2009.

James E. McWilliams

*Just Food: Where Locavores Get it Wrong and How We Can Truly Eat Responsibly.* New York: Little Brown and Company, 2009.

Marion Nestle

*Food Politics: How the Food Industry Influences Nutrition and Health.* Berkeley: University of California Press, 2007.

Robert Paarlberg

*Food Politics: What Everyone Needs to Know.* New York: Oxford University Press, 2010.

Carlo Petrini

*Slow Food Nation: Why Our Food Should Be Good, Clean, And Fair.* New York: Rizzoli Ex Libris, 2007.

Michael Pollan

*In Defense of Food: An Eater's Manifesto.* New York: Penguin Press, 2008.

Janet Poppendieck

*Free For All: Fixing School Food in America.* Berkeley: University of California Press, 2010.

Jill Richardson    *Recipe for America: Why Our Food System Is Broken and What We Can Do to Fix It.* Brooklyn, NY: Ig Publishing, 2009.

Pamela C. Ronald, Raoul W. Adamchak    *Tomorrow's Table: Organic Farming, Genetics, and the Future of Food.* New York: Oxford University Press, 2010.

Joel Salatin    *Everything I Want to Do Is Illegal: War Stories from The Local Food Front.* Swoope, VA: Polyface, 2007.

Ron Schmid    *The Untold Story of Milk: The History, Politics and Science of Nature's Perfect Food: Raw Milk from Pasture-Fed Cows.* Washington, DC: New Trends Publishing, 2009.

Karl Weber    *Food, Inc.: How Industrial Food Is Making Us Sicker, Fatter and Poorer—And What You Can Do About It.* New York: Public Affairs, 2009.

Patrick Westhoff    *The Economics of Food: How Feeding and Fueling the Planet Affects Food Prices.* FT Press, 2010.

## Periodicals

Jeri Lynn Chandler    "Bon Appétit Management Company Goes for rBGH-free Yogurt," *San Francisco Examiner*, August 4, 2010.

Paul Collier    "The Politics of Hunger," *Foreign Affairs*, November–December, 2008.

| Monica Eng | "Locavorism Expands Its Boundaries," *Chicago Tribune*, May 12, 2010. |
| Lisa Fickenscher | "Eatery Fights Calorie Police," *Crain's New York*, August 16, 2009. |
| Larry Gabriel | "Life in the Desert," *Metro Times*, September 26, 2007. |
| Amanda Gardner | "U.S. Food Safety: Home-Grown Problems Abound," *U.S. News and World Report*, January 14, 2008. |
| David Gumpert | "Is the Obama Administration About to Eat the Foodies' Lunch?" *Grist*, January 8, 2010. |
| David Gumpert | "Farmer-consumer Group Challenges FDA Authority to Ban Interstate Raw-Milk Sales," *Grist*, February 22, 2010. |
| Jim Hightower | "Food Industry Is Now Calling Junk Food 'Healthy'—Why Could That Be?" *Alternet*, September 17, 2009. |
| Joshua Kurlantzick | "The Chinavore's Dilemma," *Mother Jones*, September–October 2008. |
| Tom Laskawy | "Food Safety Reform is a Mess," *Grist*, May 7, 2010. |
| Lyndsey Layton | "Reversing Itself, FDA Expresses Concerns over Health Risks from BPA," *The Washington Post*, January 16, 2010. |

Darry Madden — "More Dairies Going Raw," *The Boston Globe*, February 23, 2008.

Michael Moss — "Food Companies Are Placing the Onus for Safety on Consumers," *The New York Times*, May 15, 2009.

Michael Moss — "The Burger That Shattered Her Life," *The New York Times*, October 3, 2009.

Michael Pollan — "Food Movement, Rising," *The New York Review of Books*, June 10, 2010.

Steven Reinberg — "Food-borne Illnesses in U.S. Cost $152B Annually," *U.S. News and World Report*, March 3, 2010.

Paul Roberts — "Spoiled: Organic and Local is So 2008," *Mother Jones*, March–April 2009.

Claire Robinson and Jonathan Matthews — "Was 2009 the Year the World Turned Against GM?" *Ecologist*, January 11, 2010.

Susanne Rust and Meg Kissinger — "FDA Relied Heavily on BPA Lobby," *Journal Sentinel*, May 16, 2009.

Angela Townsend — "Organic Food Benefits Debated in Wake of President's Report on Cancer, Environment," *The Plain Dealer*, May 18, 2010.

J. Justin Wilson — "Michelle Obama, First Nanny," *The Daily Caller*, February 12, 2010.

Jane Zang

"Lack of Adequate Records Limits FDA," *The Wall Street Journal,* March 26, 2009.

# Index